Music and Dyslexia

Music and Dyslexia

A Positive Approach

Edited by

TIM MILES
JOHN WESTCOMBE
DIANA DITCHFIELD

WILEY

Other Wiley Editorial Offices

John Wiley & Sons Inc., 111 River Street, Hoboken, NJ 07030, USA

Jossey-Bass, 989 Market Street, San Francisco, CA 94103-1741, USA

Wiley-VCH Verlag GmbH, Boschstr. 12, D-69469 Weinheim, Germany

John Wiley & Sons Australia Ltd, 42 McDougall Street, Milton, Queensland 4064, Australia

John Wiley & Sons (Asia) Pte Ltd, 2 Clementi Loop #02-01, Jin Xing Distripark, Singapore
129809

John Wiley & Sons Canada Ltd, 6045 Freemont Blvd, Mississauga, ONT, L5R 4J3, Canada

Wiley also publishes its books in a variety of electronic formats. Some content that appears
in print may not be available in electronic books.

Library of Congress Cataloguing-in-Publication Data

Data is available

British Library Cataloguing in Publication Data

A catalogue record for this book is available from the British Library

ISBN: 978-0-470-06557-0 (cloth)
ISBN: 978-0-470-06558-7 (paper)

Typeset by Aptara, New Delhi, India
Printed and bound in Singapore by Markono Print Media Pte Ltd

This book is printed on acid-free paper responsibly manufactured from sustainable forestry
in which at least two trees are planted for each one used for paper production.

Contents

Contents _____

_____

Foreword

Tim Miles and his colleagues have edited and contributed to a most useful book of essays. It will be useful not only to specialist teachers of children with dyslexia but also to many class teachers who have children with a variety of different difficulties among their pupils, for the emphasis throughout is on neurological differences between one child and another, whether these children are identified as having special needs or not. The term 'neurodiversity' is a helpful one, because it suggests that there are ways of teaching which, in the early years, will appeal to all children, whatever their developmental differences, and which they can all enjoy. The rhythm games described in Chapter 4 are especially enlightening. All children can join in and practise their 'performance', and everyone will benefit. Moreover, they can be taught by teachers without specialist music training, a huge advantage in most schools. The book is thus of great practical value.

It is also optimistic and cheerful. It is impossible not to sympathize with the horrors for a dyslexic student of Grade V theory (a horror well enough known to those who are not dyslexic). And the strategies for teaching and learning musical notation for those who are dyslexic will be eagerly read by music teachers. In many different ways, this is an excellent addition to the growing literature of dyslexia and music, and it is to be warmly welcomed.

Mary Warnock
House of Lords

List of contributors

An asterisk (*) marks a cameo writer.

Adam Apostoli is a 20-year-old undergraduate student at the University of Edinburgh, currently in his third year of a degree in Music Technology. A keen singer, Adam hopes to pursue further study in Historical Musicology and Performance following his degree.

Paula Bishop-Liebler, a doctoral student at the Institute of Education, London, is researching links between music and dyslexia. She assesses and supports dyslexics at the Dyslexia Teaching Centre, Kensington, and in a variety of conservatoires including the Royal Academy of Music, the Royal College of Music and the Guildhall School of Music and Drama.

Nigel Clarke studied at the Royal Academy of Music with Paul Patterson and won the Queen's Commendation for Excellence. He has been Composer in Residence or similar to Black Dyke Mills Band and the Alabama Wind Ensemble. Nigel has written soundtracks to a number of feature films and was nominated recently at the World Soundtrack Awards.

Diana Ditchfield studied piano performance at the Royal Irish Academy of Music, before taking degrees in Education and teaching in secondary school in the United Kingdom. Her interest in dyslexia started in the 1980s. She teaches piano at the Municipal School of Music in Limerick and is a Learning Support Tutor in Disability Services at University level.

*Margaret Howlett-Jones trained at the Froebel Institute, Roehampton, with music as her special study, and worked for seven years as a primary school teacher. Following maternity leave, she took on a number of piano pupils and became increasingly interested in dyslexia in the music-learning context, taking the RSA Diploma. She is Secretary to the British Dyslexia Association Music Committee.

Carolyn King read Biochemistry at Oxford and secured her PhD at UCL Hospital Medical School. Ten years of research were undertaken on the mechanism of action of cholera toxin. She then established an oboe-orientated second career. Happily, both of these have relevance in sight-reading. She recently completed an MA in Musical Teaching in Professional Practice at Reading University.

Michael Lea is a double bass player who graduated from the BBC Training Orchestra to CBSO and the BBC Concert Orchestra. Since moving into the freelance world, he has played in over 250 films and many famous recordings. He taught for many years at the Guildhall School of Music, and latterly has devoted time to composition.

Jenny Macmillan has an MA in Psychology for Musicians from Sheffield University. She is a Suzuki piano teacher and ESA teacher trainer in Cambridge. She gives lectures and demonstrations throughout the United Kingdom on the Suzuki approach and has contributed to several music education journals.

Olivia McCarthy graduated in Music from University College, Cork, specialising in piano performance. Since obtaining her Higher Diploma of Education, she has taught piano, state examination music and the common diploma syllabus for many years at the Municipal School of Music, Limerick City, where she is presently Head of the Piano Department.

Christine McRitchie Pratt has always been involved in teaching and music-making both in schools and privately. She writes musicals as well as playing the harp and hurdy-gurdy. Her commitment to the arts includes involvement in the ADC Theatre, Cambridge, and being a founder member of Cambridge Youth Music.

Tim Miles, OBE, MA, PhD, CPsychol., FBPS, was the first Professor of Psychology at the University of Wales, Bangor, serving from 1963 to 1987, and is now Professor Emeritus. He has published widely both on dyslexia and other topics. He is an amateur cellist.

Sheila Oglethorpe graduated from the Royal Academy of Music having studied piano, cello and singing. She taught music at primary and secondary level and now teaches privately. She does dyslexia/music consultancy at Salisbury Cathedral School. The second edition of her book

Instrumental Music for Dyslexics: A Teaching Handbook was published in 2002. She lectures for the Associated Board of the Royal Schools of Music.

Katie Overy is a Lecturer in Music at the University of Edinburgh and Co-Director of the Institute for Music in Human and Social Development. She has a long-standing interest in the role of music in human learning, with an emphasis on interdisciplinary research and the integration of research and practice.

*Pauline Poole trained as a Primary School Teacher and taught across the phase, and now lectures in a College of Further Education. She is currently finishing the OCR SpLD Diploma Units. She delights in sharing her love of singing with children, and, as a committed Christian, Pauline spends her spare time involved in children's and youth work for churches in North Hertfordshire and Albania.

Annemarie Sand trained at the Royal Academy of Music and has performed extensively with major orchestras and opera companies both here and abroad. Her repertoire covers demanding roles from Sieglinde in Wagner's *Ring Cycle* and Maria in Berg's opera *Wozzeck* to contemporary opera. She now combines her solo career with teaching.

Lauren Stewart originally studied Physiological Sciences at Oxford, but transferred from bodies to brains via neuroscience training and doctorates at UCL and Harvard. Her interest in the neuropsychology of music stems from the belief that music provides a unique window onto the human mind and brain. Her current research includes amusia (inability to make sense of musical sound) and the perceptual, cognitive and motor skills in trained musicians.

John Westcombe taught music in Inner London before taking advisory and music direction posts in three large LEAs. More recently, consultancy work has been done for Trinity College of Music and Youth Music. Current interests include concert reviewing and Chairing the British Dyslexia Association Music Committee. Heinemann published his *Careers in Music* (1997).

*Siw Wood was considered 'too hopeless at spelling' to go to secretarial college, but in fact trained at art college. She reports that dyslexia has had a huge influence on her life. Her jobs have included dental nurse, ward orderly, farm worker, PR official in a theatre, mobility assistant and chauffeur. Her main hobby is singing.

Preface

This book is a sequel to *Music and Dyslexia: Opening New Doors* (Miles and Westcombe (eds), Whurr, London, 2001). It comprises both chapters from some of the contributors to the earlier book and from other musicians as well. Those who contributed to both books are Tim Miles, John Westcombe and Diana Ditchfield (who are jointly the editors of the present book), Sheila Oglethorpe, Nigel Clarke, Michael Lea, Paula Bishop-Liebler, Annemarie Sand and Siw Wood. The new contributors are Adam Apostoli, Margaret Howlett-Jones, Carolyn King, Christine McRitchie Pratt, Katie Overy, Olivia McCarthy and Lauren Stewart. Sadly, Professor Margaret (Peggy) Hubicki, a contributor to the earlier book and a leading member of the British Dyslexia Association Music Committee, died early in 2006. Her sympathetic understanding of the difficulties experienced by many dyslexic musicians has made a lasting contribution to the field. Chapter 14 in the present book, written largely by Annemarie, pays a warm tribute to Peggy.

We have divided the book into four sections. These are entitled 'Tackling Problems', 'In and Around the Classroom', 'Strategies and Successes' and 'Science Takes Us Forward'.

In the first chapter, Tim Miles outlines the main characteristics of dyslexia and briefly mentions other developmental differences which have come to the fore in recent decades. He emphasises that the word 'difference' is more satisfactory than such words as 'anomaly', 'deficit', 'disability' and the like: one of the important messages of the book as a whole is to encourage teachers of dyslexic children and adults always to think positively. In Chapter 2, Tim calls attention to some of the things which can go wrong in the lives of dyslexics. They can happen to any of us, whether dyslexic or not, but experience suggests that dyslexics are particularly vulnerable to such things, and it is therefore important that teachers should know what to expect.

In Chapter 3, Christine McRitchie Pratt gives a comprehensive list of the visiting and school-based staff requirement regarding accessories and materials as well as good advice about direct help for dyslexics in the classroom; in Chapter 4, Katie Overy provides a selection of musical activities and games suitable in both the music and language classroom for both dyslexics and others. In Chapter 5, Olivia McCarthy and Diana Ditchfield recall a very disruptive pupil who had severe difficulties with her short-term memory whom they gradually won over to competence in piano playing through appropriate tuition in her early years; some of the writing team have then pooled their thoughts, in Chapter 6, on what might lie behind pupils' reluctance to involve themselves or seemingly miss out on the pleasures of musical participation. In Chapter 7, Sheila Oglethorpe calls attention to some of the many different ways in which music can contribute richly, and unexpectedly, to the lives of those who are dyslexic, and provides valuable case studies. In Chapter 8, Tim Miles calls attention to parallels between the teaching of musical notation and mathematical notation. Because symbols are involved, these notations may take dyslexics longer to learn, but that need not prevent them from becoming highly successful musicians or mathematicians. Diana Ditchfield, in Chapter 9, acknowledges that some young musicians have found it frustrating that, at least to find a way through the examination system, theory has to be learned and written questions answered, and welcomes the role of technology in these matters.

Next come two contributions on sight-reading, written from somewhat different angles. The chapter by Sheila Oglethorpe (Chapter 10) contains a wealth of practical advice; that by Michael Lea (Chapter 11) reports that he found memorisation when playing the guitar easier and sight-reading easier when playing the cello or double bass. He offers an ingenious neurological explanation for this based on a diagram: the cortical homunculus devised by the neurologist Wilder Penfield.

For Chapter 12, there is a straightforward setting-out of good advice from Nigel Clarke, who has needed to be very resourceful and press on against difficulties, and, in Chapter 13, there is an even-handed view, from Adam Apostoli, about how far music has been embraced by the technological age (and vice versa).

Chapter 14 relates a remarkable sequence that has a strong triangular feel about it in terms of the personalities involved, the transference of teaching expertise and the reversal of fortune. In Chapter 15, Paula Bishop-Liebler's illustrates by means of case studies the variety of skills which dyslexic singers need to accumulate according to the type of music which they wish to perform, whether, for instance, it be jazz, baroque or music for the theatre.

In Chapter 16, we hope to catch the eye in our movement between groups of musicians with 'Thirty-seven oboists'. Here, Carolyn King describes her experiences in teaching and assessing a large cohort of oboists, some but not all of whom were dyslexic. Then Jenny Macmillan, in Chapter 17, draws attention to ways in which the Suzuki influence is analogous to styles of teaching of dyslexics, not least in the matter of notation not being an essential part of that method's initial engagements, and the words 'structured', 'sequential' and 'cumulative' are shared vocabulary. In Chapter 18, Nigel Clarke's successes in both leadership of a conservatoire department and as a distinguished composer in the world of film-making demonstrate that success can be achieved and problems overcome.

In Chapter 19, Katie Overy briefly describes some of the latest brain-imaging techniques; she then outlines some research findings on the aural basis of music processing, the brain differences associated with musical training and the brain differences associated with dyslexia. In Chapter 20, Lauren Stewart provides an analysis of the various skills required for successful sight-reading; then, as a sequel to Katie's chapter, she reports on some of the studies by herself and colleagues on what has been discovered about music skills from the use of brain-imaging techniques.

Amongst the main chapters, three cameos will be found, two by individuals and the third by various hands. They serve to demonstrate the individual nature of responses to dyslexia for both young people and adults, and what teachers need to look out for.

We express our gratitude to the British Dyslexia Association for support of the Music Committee in past years. We would also like to take this opportunity to thank Joanna Westcombe for her help with the early drafts of this book.

Tim Miles, John Westcombe and Diana Ditchfield

Tackling problems

one

Dyslexia and other developmental differences

Tim Miles

Introduction

I shall start this chapter by describing briefly some of the main characteristics of dyslexia. I shall then mention other developmental differences which may be relevant in the classroom in general and to teachers of music in particular. I shall end with a brief word about diagnostic labels.

I have chosen to speak of 'differences' rather than use such terms as 'anomaly', 'deficit', 'disorder', 'handicap' and the like. It is true that in society as it exists at present dyslexics and those with other differences tend to be disadvantaged (or 'disabled') in certain specific ways. The message of this present book, however, is to encourage people to think positively: it is important both that dyslexics should not undervalue themselves and that those who teach them should encourage their strengths rather than be thinking only of their weaknesses. The Adult Dyslexia Organisation (ADO) has suggested that we should think of dyslexics not as disabled but as 'differently abled'.

The nature of dyslexia

I have always thought that the most helpful way to characterise dyslexia is to say that it is a syndrome. 'Syndrome' is a term implying a cluster of manifestations or symptoms, not necessarily identical in different individuals but showing an identifiable pattern.

In the great majority of cases, dyslexics are late in learning to read and, even with good teaching, are likely to remain poor spellers. In addition, most dyslexics have problems with short-term memory: if they have to listen to a long sentence, they may understand the early part but lose track before the end – it seems as though the amount which they can hold in mind is more limited than it is in the case of non-dyslexics. Some dyslexics show uncertainty over left and right, and a very large number have difficulty in learning their times tables (note 1.1).

It is now established that dyslexia has a physical (constitutional) basis, that is to say it arises from the way in which a person is made. This, of course, is nothing for which anyone can be blamed. The situation can be made worse by poor teaching or unsympathetic handling, but these are not the original causes of the difficulties.

It is known that dyslexia runs in families, although one sometimes comes across cases where there is no evidence of other family members being affected. It is almost certainly more common in males than in females. There is not yet agreement as to the details of what causes dyslexia. A widely held view is that dyslexics have a problem with phonology, that is with the recall and ordering of speech sounds (see in particular note 1.2). It seems likely that a major problem for most dyslexics is that of learning the correct label to attach to speech sounds – it is a problem of verbal labelling. Speech sounds are symbols and it appears to be symbols that cause dyslexics difficulty (note 1.3). Given that this is so, one would expect them to have difficulty with many different kinds of symbol, including those of mathematics and musical notation (see also Chapter 8).

If a child in your class is dyslexic, this calls for sensitivity and in particular for an awareness of when to take note of the fact. What is called for is not the abandonment of standards but a willingness to adjust one's standards so as to take into account the pupil's individual needs. As I shall show in Chapter 2, there are all kinds of things which may go wrong for the dyslexic.

Dyslexia takes a different form in different languages. In those languages where there is regular one-to-one correspondence between written letters and their sounds, learning to read and spell is not quite the problem that it is in English, where there are large numbers of so-called irregular words. For instance, the English 'yacht' is not spelled *yot* and 'neighbour' is not spelled *naber*. There are some languages, such as Welsh, Spanish and Italian, where there is a regular correspondence between the sounds that we speak and the letters that we write, and in these languages learning to read is much easier.

Other developmental differences

In this section I call attention to a number of other developmental differences which have come into prominence in the last few decades. They are: ADD (attention deficit disorder) and ADHD (attention deficit hyperactivity disorder), dyspraxia, dyscalculia and the group of disorders referred to as autistic spectrum disorders (ASD). A useful term by which to refer to all differences such as these is 'neurodiversity'. People's nervous systems are diverse – they vary; different nervous systems are advantageous – or handicapping – for different purposes. There is no clear association between these conditions and high or low intelligence, and it is most important that the abilities of those showing developmental differences should not be underestimated.

Many of the manifestations which I shall be describing occur in all of us but only in a relatively mild form. The diagnostic label is appropriate only when the problems are severe and persistent. Also one needs to bear in mind that there can sometimes be what is called 'co-morbidity': more than one diagnostic description may be applicable in the case of the same individual, for example a number of dyslexics but by no means all of them are also dyspraxic.

ADD and ADHD

Those with ADD may have particular difficulty in sustaining concentration for more than a very short period of time. Written work may give the impression of being disorganised and carelessly put together. Tasks may sometimes be abandoned before they have been completed.

In the case of ADHD, there is the additional complication of hyperactivity – continual restlessness. The person with ADHD fidgets and finds it difficult to sit still. In the case of both ADD and ADHD, the individual is liable to act on impulse without adequate consideration of the consequences. Impulsivity may manifest itself in impatience and in difficulty in delaying responses until questions have been completed. It may lead to accidents, for instance knocking objects over, bumping into people or impetuously grabbing a hot pan without working out that one will be burned. There may sometimes be engagement in potentially dangerous activities without consideration of what might be the consequences. It is possible that the condition sometimes runs in families, but, as in the case of dyslexia, this is far from being universal.

Dyspraxia

The essential feature of dyspraxia is, of course, poor motor co-ordination. In the case of children, it is sometimes known as 'developmental co-ordination disorder' (DCD) or as 'the clumsy child syndrome'. This poor motor control may lead to other effects – problems over accurate perception, speech difficulties, untidy handwriting, disorganised planning and sometimes slowness in retrieving information from print. Manifestations of dyspraxia are sometimes found among dyslexics, but this is relatively infrequent.

Dyscalculia

There is no agreement as to whether dyscalculia should be regarded as a distinct and separate syndrome or whether its manifestations are all part of the dyslexic syndrome.

There is no doubt, however, that severe and persistent problems with arithmetical calculation can regularly be found. Among them are a very small number who have few or no literacy problems. If these are variations within the dyslexia syndrome, then it would seem that some widening of the dyslexia concept is called for, so that it would be proper to call a person 'dyslexic' even in the absence of any severe reading or spelling problems.

On the other side of the coin, so to speak, there are very few dyslexics without any calculation problems. In my own research (Miles, 1997; Miles, 1993) I found that about 90% of the dyslexics whom I assessed could not recite the six-times, seven-times and eight-times tables without stumbling; and it seems common sense to suppose that dyslexics' difficulties with symbolic material should extend to mathematical symbols.

To complicate matters, there appear to be a small number of individuals who are impaired in their ability to reason mathematically, for example with matrices and block design tests, which the typical dyslexic can manage adequately.

One of the problems in this whole area is to know where to 'lump' and where to 'split', that is where to classify manifestations together as constituting the same syndrome ('lumping') and where to treat them as separate ('splitting'). Because of co-morbidity between syndromes, the whole situation is very untidy from the theoretical point of view. Provided there is careful examination of individual needs, however, this theoretical untidiness need not have an adverse effect on practice. Hopefully, advances in neurology will throw further light on the theoretical side.

Autistic spectrum disorders (ASD)

The main characteristic of autism is impaired communication with others. Those who are autistic are not easily able to understand the point of view of others and, as a consequence, they may be deficient in social skills. They may also be restricted in their use of eye-to-eye contact and may not easily be able to 'read' the significance of other people's gestures and bodily movements. Some of them may have an interest in forming friendships but these may not always be maintained; this may be due to their inability to understand other people's needs. Some autistic people have a restricted repertoire of activities and interests and keep returning to the same routines without attempting anything new.

Asperger's syndrome is thought to be a less severe form of autism – and again manifests itself in the inability to see the other person's point of view. Some of those with Asperger's syndrome are liable to miss out on the subtleties of language and take what is said entirely literally. One of the leaflets of the Asperger's Society describes someone who misinterpreted the expression 'She bit my head off'. I myself had the following two experiences: a student told me that he had recently photocopied a number of pages from a library book. I was unsure of the copyright regulations and wished to make clear that I did not wish to be associated with what he had done. I therefore said, 'I am rather deaf.' With a look of concern on his face the student said, 'Oh, I am so sorry.' In contrast another student, who had none of these developmental differences, asked if she could attend one of my lectures even though at the time she was not registered as a student. It would have been churlish to refuse, but to cover myself I mischievously said, 'I am rather short-sighted.' She got the message and attended the lecture. A few weeks later, wanting to attend another of my lectures, she came up to me and asked, 'Are you short-sighted again this morning?'

On the use of diagnostic labels

One sometimes hears it said that it is wrong to *label* children, whether as dyslexic, dyspraxic or anything else. I have never been able to subscribe to this view.

The correct diagnostic label is essential if the individual concerned is to be adequately helped. If correct diagnostic labels are not used, teachers are more than likely to act upon their own incorrect ones. I remember one occasion when an official said at a meeting on dyslexia, 'We don't label children' – and was greeted by an indignant mother who said, 'My son prefers the label "dyslexic" to the label "dumbo".' This provoked thunderous applause.

We should always remember, however, that, although those who carry a particular diagnostic label may have much in common, their needs may be different, particularly at different times of their lives. Within those who carry a particular diagnostic label there should never be a one-size-fits-all treatment.

Notes

Note 1.1. For further documentation of these claims the reader may wish to consult Miles (1993) and Miles (2006).

Note 1.2. For further discussion of the significance of phonological deficits in dyslexia see Snowling (2000) and Snowling and Hulme (2006).

Note 1.3. A colleague, Professor Nick Ellis, devised an ingenious series of experiments which suggested that if non-symbolic material were presented dyslexics performed no worse than controls. What he did was to adapt for use with dyslexics a procedure which had been devised independently by a psychologist named Posner. In our experiment the subjects were dyslexic and control children aged between 10 and 15 years. The stimuli were pairs of letters of the alphabet. The task was to press one key if the members of the pair were the same and to press another key if they were different. Sometimes the stimuli were two upper-case letters, for example OO, RR (same) or OB, RM (different); this was termed the 'visual match' condition. Sometimes, however, a capital letter was placed alongside a lower-case letter, for instance Bb, Mm (same) or Ba, Mb (different); this was referred to as the 'name match' condition. It was found that in the visual match condition the dyslexic subjects were not significantly slower than the controls in making the decision but that they were consistently slower in the name match condition. The order of magnitude was not all that great (between a tenth and a fifth of a second) but it held up consistently. A brief summary of this research will be found in Miles (2006, pp. 78–79). A similar difference in subjects' responses to symbolic and non-symbolic material was found in the Kannada language (Miles, 2006, pp. 88–89).

Note 1.4. A brief account of ADHD, Asperger's syndrome and dyspraxia will be found in Du Pre *et al.* (2007, Chapter 2). For those interested in neurodiversity, the BRAIN HE project, led by David Pollack at de Montford University, Leicester, aims to provide thorough and up-to-date information from organisations which support neurodiversity in all its different forms. In this connection see www.brainhe.com.

Further information

Overviews of the dyslexia field will be found in Thomson (1991) and in Miles and Miles (1999). Other information relevant to this chapter will be found in Miles (2004), which is an edited book on the stresses experienced by many dyslexics, and in Miles and Miles (2004), which is an edited book on the mathematical difficulties experienced by dyslexics. Accounts of the many ways in which dyslexia affects the lives of musicians will be found in Miles and Westcombe (2001).

The Bangor Dyslexia Test (Miles, 1997) is available on the open market from Learning Development Aids, Duke Street, Wisbech, Cambs PE13 2AE. This test was used by Carolyn King (see Chapter 16) in testing 37 oboists, some of whom were showing clear signs of dyslexia.

Dyslexic teenagers or dyslexic adults who are considering going into higher education may like to consult Du Pre *et al.* (2007). Those interested in research studies may wish to consult *Dyslexia: An International Journal of Research and Practice*, published by John Wiley & Sons (Chichester), and *Annals of Dyslexia*, published by the International Dyslexia Association, Chester Building Suite 382, 8600 LaSalle Road, Baltimore MD 21285-2044, USA.

For advice on dyslexia, readers may like to write to the Adult Dyslexia Association, 336 Brixton Road, London SW9 7AA, to the British Dyslexia Association, 98 London Road, Reading RG1 5AU and/or to Dyslexia Action, Wick House, Park Road, Egham, Surrey TW20 0HH. The address of the National Autistic Society is: 393 City Road, London EC4 1NE.

References

Du Pre, E.A., Gilroy, D.E. and Miles, T.R. (2007) *Dyslexia at College* (3rd edn), RoutledgeFalmer, London.

Miles, T.R. (1993) *Dyslexia: The Pattern of Difficulties*, Whurr, London.

Miles, T.R. (2006) *Fifty Years in Dyslexia Research*, John Wiley & Sons, Chichester.

Miles, T.R. (ed) (2004) *Dyslexia and Stress* (2nd edn), Whurr, London.

Miles, T.R. (1997) *The Bangor Dyslexia Test*, Learning Development Aids, Wisbech, Cambs.

Miles, T.R. and Miles, E. (eds) (2004) *Dyslexia and Mathematics*, RoutledgeFalmer, London.

Miles, T.R. and Miles, E. (1999) *Dyslexia: A Hundred Years On* (2nd edn), Open University Press, Ballmoor, Bucks.

Miles, T.R. and Westcombe, J. (eds) (2001) *Music and Dyslexia: Opening New Doors*, Whurr, London.

Snowling, M.J. (2000) *Dyslexia* (2nd edn), Blackwell, Oxford.

Snowling, M.J. and Hulme, C. (2006) *The Science of Reading: A Handbook*, Blackwell, Oxford.

Thomson, M.E. (1991) *Developmental Dyslexia* (3rd edn), Whurr, London.

two

Things that can go wrong

Tim Miles

Introduction

All of us will have experienced mishaps and embarrassments at various times in our lives. I should like to suggest, however, that in this respect dyslexics are particularly vulnerable. The descriptions in this chapter range from minor mishaps to serious embarrassments. I cannot promise that every episode took place exactly as I describe them here, but they are all the kinds of thing that can occur particularly in the lives of dyslexics.

The obvious problems of the dyslexic are well known – the frustrations when they first go to school and find that other members of the class are so much more successful than they are at deciphering those unintelligible marks on paper which others call 'writing'.

Quite apart from such things, however, there are many mishaps – not necessarily anyone's fault – which nevertheless may cause embarrassment and sometimes hurt. Dyslexia affects all aspects of life, not just reading and spelling. The following are some examples.

Social situations

A dyslexic adult whom I assessed told me that he had been invited to a party where he knew that they would play word games (solving anagrams etc.). He also knew that he would not be able to cope; so he excused himself from joining in by appearing with his arm in a sling and saying that he could not write because he had broken his wrist. What he had forgotten was that some six months earlier, with the same group of people, he had produced the same excuse. When he now used it on this second occasion, great was his embarrassment when his hostess said to him in surprise: 'What? Have you broken your wrist again?' He told me he felt a complete fool.

A number of us were enjoying a humorous cartoon. In the cartoon some police officers were approaching a building and the caption underneath said: 'He's got a gnu' – and a picture showed a man and a gnu side by side. A dyslexic member of our party said: 'I don't see what is funny. Why is "He's got a gun" funny?' We had to explain that she had misread what was in fact the word 'gnu'. I blamed myself for not foreseeing the embarrassment which this misreading might cause.

Another dyslexic adult had had to give up playing darts. The reason: he was slow at calculating, and this became an embarrassment when his mates knew instantly what number he needed for his next throw but he himself needed time to work the sum out.

A successful dyslexic businessman had been honoured by being appointed Chairman of the Guild. At the initiation ceremony he suddenly heard the words: 'I call on our new chairman to read the rules of the guild.' He knew he was incapable of reading aloud, and, pleading illness, he went off home and did not dare to face the members of the guild again. They, in their turn, considered that he had treated them with extreme discourtesy.

A dyslexic adult was working in an office where there was always a large amount of noise. This noise prevented him from concentrating. At first, when he asked to be moved to a quieter room, his employer thought he was just being tiresome, while a fellow employee complained that it was wrong that he should receive some special treatment not given to his workmates. Only when it was explained that some dyslexics cannot easily work during a buzz of conversation was it appreciated that the request was a reasonable one.

'Left' and 'right'

A dyslexic child brought up as a Roman Catholic regularly needed to cross herself. This, of course, involved combining getting the order correct with remembering which was 'right' and which was 'left'; she told me that she found this very difficult.

I have assessed several children who, according to their parents, found it difficult to put the knives, forks and spoons in the correct place when laying the table. If one has been told that the fork goes on the left, it is still necessary to know not only which is the fork – no difficult task on its own for a dyslexic of sufficient age – but which side is the 'left'. This again appears to be a case of having to remember too many things at the same time.

On one occasion slowness in working out 'left' and 'right' had serious consequences. A medical student was taking an examination where the questions were multiple choice. The examination was timed, and the instructions were that if X is true tick the box on the right, and if Y is true tick the box on the left. This student assured me that he knew all the answers: he failed the examination because he completed only half the questions – chiefly because of the time it took him to work out which box was 'right' and which was 'left'. Thus a potentially able doctor was lost to the medical profession.

Time management

A headmaster arranged to see one of his dyslexic pupils at 11.30 a.m. The dyslexic pupil, however, mistook the time and turned up for the appointment at 11 a.m. There was no sign of the headmaster. He waited for 20 minutes and then, deciding that the headmaster was not coming, walked away. The headmaster duly appeared at 11.30 and was far from pleased when he found that the boy did not arrive at 11.30.

I am told that, in the past, if a young man on probation failed to keep an appointment with his probation officer severe penalties routinely followed. It is now recognised that a dyslexic who is on probation may miss an appointment not because of unwillingness to co-operate but simply because of a deficient sense of time.

There are times when the behaviour of a dyslexic makes one really indignant. Here is an account of something which I experienced at first hand. A 13-year-old girl had been receiving tuition from one of our Dyslexia Unit teachers. Her family were very short of money, and I had arranged for her to receive some financial help from our (very impoverished) hardship fund. Picture my dismay and indignation when her teacher told me that on the last two occasions she had been three-quarters of an hour late for her lesson. Not surprisingly, I was furious: considering that the girl was being paid for out of our scarce funds, surely she ought to have the common courtesy to turn up on time? However, I happened to be around on the day when she was next due to have her lesson – and she arrived half an hour early. Then the penny dropped, and I suggested to her teacher that she should teach the girl to tell the time!

Travelling

A famous actor had been asked to attend a play reading. He lost his way and failed to turn up on time. The other actors, not knowing that he was dyslexic, supposed he was too arrogant to take the trouble to turn up on time. He reported to me that, once the nature of his dyslexia had been explained to him, he 'felt forgiven'.

A dyslexic adult wanted to visit the British Museum. There was, in fact, a sign to it nearby which she had not noticed. She therefore asked a passer-by for directions. He turned to her rather angrily and said: 'Why can't you read the bloody notice?'

A dyslexic driver had been supplied with a route map; her husband became very cross at her slowness in orientating this map and this crossness caused a further confusion over 'left' and 'right'.

Another dyslexic driver stopped to ask directions from a passer-by. The answer was given at great speed – as it might be: 'Second turn on the left; then go on for 200 yards until you come to the church and then turn right...' – by which time the driver was so confused that he could remember nothing.

Another dyslexic, because of her uncertainty over 'left' and 'right', had devised a compensatory strategy: 'turn left' meant turn where there is no on-coming traffic; 'turn right' meant turning to the side where the road is clear after there has been on-coming traffic. This strategy worked well enough – until she had to drive a car in the United States of America, where they drive on the right-hand side of the road.

There can also be problems for a dyslexic who travels by public transport. Two dyslexic teenagers, unfamiliar with London, wanted to reach Kensington. They jumped into a tube train, which they supposed to be going there, and later found that they had landed up at Kennington, many miles further south.

If one has to catch a train, one has to identify its time of departure in terms of the 24-hour clock. This is what one dyslexic adult reported: 'If I've got to go for a train, I really struggle because I often get the numbers the wrong way round and get the train time wrong.' Bus numbers may also be confusing. To quote another dyslexic adult: 'I have to be very careful with 6s and 9s. Certain numbers I will switch. I can see the figures 42 in front of me and write them correctly, but when I speak I may say: "24".'

Dyslexics who feel insecure in general may find their insecurities compounded when they have to travel. I heard recently of a dyslexic musician who had had to travel from London to Exeter and had been told to change at Reading. On reaching Reading, however, as a result of listening to an announcement on a loudspeaker, she suddenly panicked, thinking she was on the wrong platform. Although she eventually arrived safely at Exeter, the journey had been extremely stressful.

Conclusion

It follows from all this that there are circumstances where waxing indignant is not very helpful. Once one knows that a person is dyslexic, their behaviour can sometimes be seen in a new light. The office worker who was disturbed by noise was not just being selfish: like quite a number of dyslexics he needed extra peace and quiet in order to function effectively. The actor who was considered arrogant in fact felt scared and guilty. The girl who was late for her lessons was not just being cussed or careless – she needed to be taught how to tell the time. A positive approach to all happenings of this kind is likely to be more effective and to make dyslexics happier and less stressed than blaming them and finding fault with them.

I am grateful to Helen Arkell, Sheila Oglethorpe and Deborah Lamont for supplying me with some of the material which has been used in this chapter. For further information on the problems experienced by dyslexics when they travel see Lamont and Lyons (2007).

Reference

Lamont, D. and Lyons, G. (2007) *Understanding and Addressing Dyslexia in Travel Information Provision*. Paper 2A1.12. Published at the Universities Transport Studies Group Annual Conference.

Cameo One

Troubles with the stave?

Siw Wood

In the earlier book (Miles and Westcombe, 2001), I explain that my memory problems mean that I cannot remember note placements without counting up laboriously from middle C. When I learn something, I usually remember it for life – no problem. However, I have never been able to master mnemonics, a helpful memory aid for the dyslexic, and this has been a problem.

I also said that God having made me dyslexic, He was also kind and made me a top soprano; so I don't have to fight my way through the jungle of the stave to read my line.

Recently, at an opera course, I was given a second soprano part by an unsympathetic assistant director. The only way I could learn this was to enlarge the pages to A3, white out the German words, highlight the English words and finally white out the first soprano's notes. All my life, I've sung 'first'!

In a mad moment I bought a small Celtic harp, with the hope of learning to accompany folk songs in a like-minded group. I found the technique of playing not that hard and was helped by the Cs being red and the Fs black, together with the right-hand/treble-clef relationship at least being familiar. However, having to unravel the bass-clef/left-hand mysteries meant that I had to spend so much time struggling with that, that I couldn't get the fingers to complete the sequence.

At the moment, I can't afford lessons, and am thinking of swapping teachers to one who will teach the traditional Welsh aural method, where the good ear virtually removes the necessity for fluency in reading notation. But I may still have problems.

Some people ask whether I dance. I may learn the first two or three sequences, but add four and five, and one and two have fled my brain.

I do hope that this doesn't happen to my harp playing.

Wish me luck!

Reference

Miles, T.R. and Westcombe, J. (eds) (2001) *Music and Dyslexia: Opening New Doors*, Whurr, London.

In and around the classroom

three

In and around the classroom

Christine McRitchie Pratt

The music room can be a rewarding place when things go well, but they will not always go well. This chapter is divided into two parts. The first part introduces some strategies that may help the dyslexic student (of any age!) when things go awry. The second part is made up of several lists that teachers might find helpful when teaching dyslexic students.

Singing

Most schools provide their pupils with an opportunity to sing, even if it is just singing hymns in assembly (and that often to a CD). Place the dyslexic pupil in the front row and next to a good strong singer. If an overhead projector or PowerPoint is being used, ensure that the text is clear, the verses are clearly numbered and that verse and chorus are clearly delineated, and use a coloured background wherever possible. If the student can have their own copy, possibly on coloured paper, well spaced and with a larger font, so much the better. Read the words through with everyone first and explain any anomalies (for example old-fashioned language or abbreviations).

Board work/worksheets

- There is a place for 'chalk and talk'. Use different colours for different lines or ideas, and use bullet points. Please make sure the writing is legible and that the student has a clear view of the board. Revisit all the time.

- Worksheets must be clear and uncluttered. Blue, yellow or pink paper may be preferred. Let the student choose. Choose a clear, unfussy font.

Performing using notation

- Highlight a part to make it clearer. Use arrows to show change to new line. Arrow Post-its are now widely available.
- Highlight a particular sequence and colour unexpected notes (e.g. accidentals) or odd fingerings, similarly with instructions (dynamics/repeats etc.). Ask the student for their choice of colour – they will feel more included.
- Use musical 'spectacles' for 'LOOK OUT'!
- Check that the task has been understood.

Listening/watching

- Make sure the dyslexic student understands the task and what they are listening/watching out for.
- Place them away from distractions.
- In the case of watching a screen, position them at the front and straight in front – prime position!

In general

- Differentiation is the name of the game.
- Use lots of multisensory and kinaesthetic approaches and strategies.
- Use clapping/human drum kit/mnemonics/aide memoires such as:
  Every Good Band Deserves Fans!
  Always Come Early, Grandma
- Organisational and timing skills are often a problem
  - suggest pupils make a credit-card size reminder of things to do
  - check that the medium-term targets are in sight, and eventually achieved

- check that non-music matters (like the law regarding photocopying) are taken into account
- Revisit frequently
  - always err on the side of commending good work
  - let it be known that you appreciate hard work, even if it does not always bring brilliant results
- Find something the student is good at (e.g. ostinato) and make it their special thing.

Always praise!

Notes for teachers: Are *you* ready for the lesson?

These lists are designed to help both visiting and school-based staff. Clearly, not everyone can carry everything around with them, but much time can be wasted through not having emergency supplies.

Before the lesson

Ensure you have:

- pencils, sharpeners, erasers
- coloured pencils, felt tips, highlighter pens
- Post-its of different sizes and colours (for easy access to music in books and for messages)
- manuscript paper
- reward stickers for all ages.

As well as:

- copies of all the music and accompaniments your pupils are using
- CD/tape machine (especially useful for vocal accompaniments to work with)

- appropriate sight-reading and aural tests
- duets and fun music.

You will also need tools of the trade, such as:

- valve oil, through rosin and peg paste
- spare reeds
- emergency spike holders
- screwdrivers and dusters.

Check your store weekly!

During the lesson

- Always give a warm welcome and smile and use the pupil's name.
- Engage with your pupil; make sure that they look at you.
- Check your pupil has understood each instruction – if not, repeat it and, if this does not work, come from another angle and explain it in a different way.
- Write careful, legible and *brief* notes in a practice notebook at the end of every lesson – vocalise as you write and check that your pupil has understood the instructions. Do not forget to put in the time, date and, if necessary, the place of the next lesson.
- Practice charts can help, plus a reward system.

Please be:

- consistent, interesting and interested (your lesson may be the only one-to-one session that the pupil has – we are in a privileged position)
- lively and always make sure some music is worked on (but do not give too many instructions in one go).

Multisensory approaches

- Even scales can be interesting: sing, hum or whistle them. Make thinking up ways for your pupil to memorise notes and fingerings fun.
- Pace the patterns around the room: long step – major interval, short step – minor interval.
- Note the arpeggio within the scale while playing (e.g. stamp a foot).

- With the pupil, play in canon/contrary motion/thirds etc.
- Use some of the patterns from the Associated Board jazz syllabus.
- Look at the title of the piece and ask your pupil to describe the feeling it should have (e.g. happy/sad/marching/dancing).
- Younger pupils will enjoy making the appropriate faces or sounds on their instruments.
- Ask your pupil to make an illustration of the title.
- Ask what colours they see in the music – add these to the copy if it helps.
- Check that all instructions given at the start of the music are understood. If not, illustrate them physically (within reason!) and ask your pupil to do the same and to highlight them (I still remember my wonderful trumpet teacher walking round the room in a steadfast manner to give the idea of andante – I still do it today).
- Check that all other instructions, such as repeats, 1st and 2nd time bars, da capo, dal segno, coda, general pause and volte subito are understood and the Italian words known. Always use colour and highlight pens to help.
- With guitars and keyboards, it may help to highlight chord sequences and patterns (this also applies to stringed instruments when using different positions). Always ask your pupil to choose the colour and, when time permits, let them do the inscribing themselves.

Be aware that there may be:

- difficulties with sorting out left or right hands (which hand do you write with? – no problem if it is with the right; otherwise, a trendy armband may help); do not insist on dealing with left and right if 'this hand' and 'that hand' will achieve the same results
- problems with fingering – pianists and harpists use five fingers on each hand numbered from one to five, the thumb being one, while most other instruments use thumb plus one, two, three and four; use other terminology, such as 'little finger' (the 'pinkie' in the United States) or 'ring finger', until confidence is gained
- misunderstanding with instructions for higher and lower, particularly with a stringed instrument; similarly with instructions for up and down.

Don't forget: black on white glares

- Photocopy onto pale-coloured paper, such as yellow, pink and blue, and work with the colour your pupil finds makes the notes the clearest.
- Enlarge if necessary.

After all that, learning the music is easy!

The voice

- Very few children are tone deaf; they have just not had the help they need. They can all talk!
- Work from a note your pupil can home in on and then gradually extend in both directions.
- Illustrate intervals and, later, letter names using the beginnings of well-known songs (1–2, *Happy Birthday*, 1–5, *Twinkle, Twinkle, Little Star*).
- Always do a vocal warm-up, using movement if possible. When teaching new music, use call and response and always teach the chorus before the verse.

Getting a sense of rhythm and timing: not so easy!

- Ask pupils to clap to tunes they know. Start with clapping on the first beat, then second and so on.
- Similarly, ask them to stamp or vocalise using the same pattern.
- Put all the patterns together to make a human drum-kit (e.g. 1. stamp, 2. clap, 3. click fingers, 4. shout).
- Use popular words and phrases to help with rhythm patterns (e.g. Olympic Games, Manchester United, Panathaniakos – Greek football team, good for six-eight!); words like 'strawberry' and 'hippopotamus' work well for ornaments.

Dealing with problems outside the classroom

- These may be with other pupils or at home.
- The one-to-one ratio enjoyed by music staff may mean they are the first to notice unusual behaviour or tension.
- Schools have procedures for dealing with pupils going through a bad patch.
- Who you pass this concern on to will depend on the nature of your employment in the school.

After the lesson

- Log continuing problems (coming late or without instrument) but also achievements.
- If there are consistent problems, talk to the appropriate staff member.
- If there are obvious difficulties either with reading music or physically, there may well be dyslexic or dyspraxic tendencies, but perhaps they just need an eye test!

However:

- not all dyslexics have problems reading music
- many non-dyslexics do; so we must teach accordingly
- it will be important to separate the possibility of difficulty with notation from that of suitability of instrument
- the teacher must ask themselves: is the instrument the right one for the child (see Chapter 6).

It has been well said that if your pupil does not learn the way you teach, you must teach in the way they learn.

Music is for life. It must be purposeful, rewarding and fun!

GREAT QUOTE

four

Classroom rhythm games for literacy support

Katie Overy

Introduction

It is increasingly recognised that engagement with music can support the acquisition of language skills. This chapter describes a collection of musical games designed specifically for dyslexic children and aimed at phonological development. The activities focus on auditory and motor timing skills and are intended for small groups of children, but can be developed and adapted for other circumstances as appropriate. In a small-scale research study, the games were found to lead to improvements in rhythm skills, phonological skills and spelling skills.

Music and language

Music and language are very different kinds of human communication, used for very different purposes. However, there are also some striking similarities between music and language, since both communicate via complex, highly structured and culturally specific sequences of auditory units, both take place in time, and thus require sustained attention and memory in order to process and interpret incoming information, and both develop naturally in infants but require hundreds of hours of training in order to achieve literacy. Considering these shared characteristics, it is perhaps not surprising to learn that abilities in music and language have been found to correlate or that trained musicians have been found to show strengths in verbal skills (for example Slevc and Miyake, 2006; Chan *et al.*, 1998). Recent neuroscience research has even shown that music and language employ shared brain regions (see Chapter 20, this volume).

Such research findings lend strong support to claims from practitioners that music can have a positive influence on children's language skills. Music educators, for example, have suggested that singing is a particularly valuable tool in the language classroom and music therapists have advocated the use of singing for children with language disabilities (for example Kolb, 1996; Sutton, 1995). Meanwhile, developmental psychologists have noted the sing-song nature of infant-directed speech and the universality of infant-directed singing, suggesting these may be extremely important in the development of human language skills (for example Trevarthen, 1999). This range of anecdotal and experimental evidence is compelling in its variety and suggests that dyslexic children might also benefit from musical experience.

Dyslexia and timing

Dyslexia, of course, presents a special case of language disability, the precise nature and cause of which remain under intense investigation and discussion. Particular difficulties with phonological skills are well established, but there are many theories as to why these difficulties occur. Examining this literature from a musical perspective, it is interesting to note that there is a strong emphasis on temporal processing deficits and timing deficits, particularly in the auditory and motor domains. For example, studies have found that dyslexia can affect the rapid temporal processing of auditory stimuli, the rapid naming of pictures, judging whether a tone is longer or shorter than a previous tone, rhythmic finger tapping and detecting the rhythmic stress patterns of speech (for example Tallal *et al.*, 1993; Nicolson *et al.*, 1995; Wolf and Bowers, 2000; Goswami *et al.*, 2002). Musical timing skills have also often been noted as a potential area of difficulty, both by experimental psychologists and by music educators (for example Oglethorpe, 1996; Overy, 2003).

Interestingly, there are also indications that emphasising the temporal aspects of language might be useful for dyslexic children. For example, it has been shown that spelling performance can be improved by learning to tap out the number of syllables in a word and that auditory training using slowed-down speech stimuli can lead to improved phonological skills (Habib *et al.*, 2002). Blythe (1998) proposes that singing is a natural way of slowing down speech signals and suggests that singing is beneficial for dyslexic children. It is also well established that children's knowledge of nursery rhymes (involving rhythmic singing) is strongly related to their phonological awareness (MacLean *et al.*, 1987). Such findings suggest that the development of rhythm skills and singing skills might be valuable elements of musical training for dyslexic children.

Developing a musical activities programme for dyslexic children

The idea that musical experience might be used to support dyslexic children's language and literacy skills was originally developed in an MA dissertation and subsequently led to PhD research focusing on the role of musical timing skills (Overy, 1997, 2002). Throughout the course of this research, a primary aim became the development of a programme of musical activities designed especially for dyslexic children, based on rhythm games and singing games and taking dyslexia-related strengths and weaknesses into account. It was proposed that such a programme would focus on specific problem areas such as musical timing while allowing for potential difficulties with concentration, sequencing, motor co-ordination and memorisation. In addition, particular attention would be given to techniques known to be important for dyslexic children, such as multisensory learning, carefully staged skill development and regular repetition.

In order to design such a programme, a number of different approaches to music education, music therapy and literacy support were examined, such as Johansen Sound Therapy (Johansen, 2000) and Ladders to Literacy (O'Connor *et al.*, 1998). Finally, three different music education approaches were selected for more thorough investigation: *Growing with Music* (Stocks and Maddocks, 1992), Education Through Music (ETM) (Richards, 1977) and *Earwiggo Again – Rhythm Games* (West and Holdstock, 1985). These were chosen for a variety of reasons, including their emphasis on musical learning as a positive, group experience for children of all abilities, their focus on musical participation rather than music listening or instrumental training, their use of activities that can be led by non-specialists and for their underlying philosophies on the potential of musical engagement to lead to valuable learning in other domains. A detailed review of these methods is given below, in order to explain the principles and influences behind the resulting musical activities programme.

Review of selected approaches to music education

Growing with Music

Growing with Music (Stocks and Maddocks, 1992) is a teaching method based on group singing and is highly influenced by the Kodály approach to music education[1]. Each music lesson is centred upon one or more songs, which are manipulated in various playful ways and then discussed using concepts such as rhythm, pitch and form. Singing is considered a valuable tool because teachers can learn it quickly, it is cheap and easy to organise with the minimum of disruption to the classroom and can be used to teach almost all aspects of the music curriculum. Developing a large repertoire of songs is also considered to be a good way to develop memory skills, while the physical activities used with songs are believed to help develop co-ordination and the automatisation of skills.

The method places particular emphasis on the need for aural understanding of a concept before any degree of theoretical understanding is attempted. This is considered crucial to the learning process; so a primary aim of the programme is to help children think about music for themselves, with activities and discussions helping children to discover concepts such as pulse, dynamics or tempo within the music that is familiar to them. Emphasis is also given to the carefully structured progression from one level of understanding to the next, continually consolidating what has already been learned.

The pedagogical approach is aimed at keeping the children interested and stimulated by constantly changing the focus to different aspects of the song, using activities such as counting the number of phrases, counting the number of pitches or concentrating on performance aspects, such as breathing, posture and dynamics. In addition, a song is often broken up into sections so that smaller groups of children or even soloists can sing to each other. Solo singing is treated as an ordinary activity, and is expected in every child, often incorporated into games so that the child is not conscious of their individual exposure.

[1] The Kodály approach to music education was developed in Hungary in the 1950s, and has since been adapted in more than 50 different countries around the world. The approach is based on classroom singing of folk songs and classical music, and has a highly structured curriculum that leads very quickly to musical literacy. It has often been reported that this approach leads to improvements in other areas of the school curriculum, including language skills (e.g. Hurwitz *et al.*, 1975).

In many respects then, *Growing with Music* is very appropriate for dyslexic children. It uses simple songs that everyone can enjoy together regardless of ability, and yet it focuses on the detailed, repetitive and explicit teaching of musical concepts and skills. It also shifts the focus of attention frequently between short but related activities, allowing even those with short attention spans to stay interested and involved. In addition, it places a large emphasis on ensuring aural understanding before introducing new terminology, and it involves many physical activities, which are good for motor skill development as well as simple energy release and relaxation.

Education Through Music

Education Through Music (ETM) (Richards, 1977) is an approach to primary education developed in California by Mary Helen Richards, after she visited Hungary and was inspired by discussions with Zoltán Kodály. The basic premise of the approach is that musical song games can provide a medium for the development and enhancement of both personal skills and learning skills. It is believed that, through a blend of music, movement, thinking and interaction, the children can 'enhance their natural learning process', heighten their perceptual awareness and increase their attention span, while improving their social awareness, interaction skills and self-confidence. Specific emphasis is placed on the development of perceptual skills, attention, eye–hand motor skills, general gross- and fine-motor skills, problem-solving, analysing and decision-making, along with turn-taking, sharing, listening, discussing and laughing.

The pedagogical philosophy of ETM is to let a child's natural curiosity, motivation, behaviour and stage of learning development take the lead. The concept of 'play' is considered crucial to the learning process, as it allows children to think, experiment and create in a relaxed, non-judgemental environment. The children are not taught in a traditional classroom way; they are taught in a quasi-playground way that is considered to be a more natural learning process and more likely to lead to genuine interest and concentration. The teacher or leader sings the song and explains the game and then the song is repeated while the game is played. The children slowly pick up the song and join in spontaneously, as their motivation dictates. No child is ever told to sing, they are only invited to join in the game, often through turn-taking. Non-participation is accepted, and thus it is the leader's responsibility to ensure that the activities are interesting, so that the children want to be involved. Many activities involve asking the children for their own ideas (such as choosing an action for a particular word in a song), which encourages them to participate.

The advantages of this method for dyslexic children are self-evident: the relaxed and supportive learning environment, the value placed on everyone's contribution, the opportunities for creativity and the emphasis on motor auditory co-ordination, which is often combined with visual activities (such as drawing a pattern to a song). By observing ETM sessions conducted with children who had never experienced them before, I was able to witness the changing behaviour of certain children in the group, as a result of the musical games and activities. For example, those who were less able and perhaps less comfortable in a group slowly became more confident and involved, contributing more often and more happily. Meanwhile, the children who were initially attention-seeking, over-talkative or disruptive gradually learned to take their turn, listen to others and take an interest in their contribution, while thoroughly enjoying the limelight when it came to their turn. The genuine sense of playfulness combined with the lack of fear of being wrong seemed very powerful, and musical involvement and development were quick to appear.

Earwiggo

Earwiggo (West and Holdstock, 1984, 1985) is a collection of booklets of songs and musical games produced by the Yorkshire and Humberside Association for Music in Special Education (YHAMSE). Musical expertise is not considered necessary to lead the music sessions; enthusiasm is emphasised as the most important quality to bring to any musical activity. Throughout Yorkshire and Humberside, YHAMSE organises meetings, workshops and courses for people who are involved with children with learning difficulties (such as teachers and parents), along with workshops and music festivals for the children themselves.

There are five booklets in the *Earwiggo* collection, each of which deals with a different aspect of musical skill: *Listening Games*, *Rhythm Games*, *Pitch Games*, *Chord Book* and *Note Book*. The activities described in the booklets were developed by the authors through playing the games with classes of children with learning difficulties. Each booklet begins with very simple activities and gradually moves to more advanced games that require more co-ordination and concentration. The activities are recommended as particularly suitable for children with special needs, but are also adaptable to cater for larger numbers of infant or junior classes.

Many of the activities from *Earwiggo Again – Rhythm Games* are particularly suited for dyslexic children, since they are designed for children who do not pick up rhythms naturally. They begin with extremely simple activities, which are usually incorporated into games in order to make them interesting and enjoyable. The activities are also designed to be flexible, allowing the leader to develop their own versions of each game, according to the needs of a particular group of children. Beginning with simple games allows children to enjoy a great deal of success, which can quickly lead to confidence, enthusiasm and a greater will to concentrate on more complex activities. Many useful activities were taken from *Earwiggo* for use in the beginning stages of the musical activities programme.

Design of the Musical Activities Programme

Aims

While the ultimate goal of the musical activities programme was to support the development of language and literacy skills, the more immediate aim was, of course, to improve musical skills, and particularly musical timing skills. Thus, the design of the programme was centred on selecting musical games that would enable dyslexic children to overcome any musical difficulties and become comfortable with fluent, shared musical experiences, paving the way for more advanced musical learning. In order to achieve this, consideration was given to the wealth of ideas from the music education methods described above, in addition to the literature described at the opening of this chapter. The resulting focus of the programme is summarised below.

Musical materials and approach

- rhythm games and song games
- actions requiring well-timed physical co-ordination
- progression from short activities to longer activities
- regular repetition, with slight developments
- progression from extremely simple to more complex activities
- encouragement of individual performance

Musical aims

- listening carefully
- singing in time with other singers
- tapping with the pulse of a song
- tapping with the rhythm of a song
- keeping in time with other musicians
- discriminating between different rhythmic patterns
- copying a rhythmic pattern
- automatising all of the above skills

Non-musical aims

- playful, enjoyable, shared musical experiences
- serious concentration and effort
- comfortable contributions with no fear of embarrassment
- personal appreciation of own abilities and ideas

Conducting the games

The initial employment of the musical activities programme was as part of an intervention study examining its potential effect on language and literacy skills. However, the sessions were always presented and conducted in the spirit of musical fun; each activity was introduced as a game and the children (aged 7 to 11) were encouraged to laugh and make jokes. Silly comments and 'creative alternatives to the rules' were incorporated into the sense of fun wherever possible and in most cases this relaxed attitude reduced the impact of any attempted bad behaviour and encouraged the children to contribute wholeheartedly and humorously. Full attention was demanded at all times, and any talking or behaviour unrelated to the activity was intercepted with questions or requests related to the musical activities. As time went on, silence became one of the rules of many of the games, with penalties for interrupting. Interruptions were always treated as outside the rules of the game, rather than as bad behaviour. In order to capture and keep all the children's undivided attention, great efforts were made to keep the games moving, with no pauses.

This style of teaching demanded a great deal of flexibility, depending on the skills, dynamics and behaviour of the group. Sometimes the children were focused and concentrated, and during these sessions they learned a great deal, gaining visible satisfaction from their achievements (from clapping difficult rhythms to simply enjoying the smooth running of a musical game). On other days the children were easily distracted and less concentrated, leading to a lack of progress, frustration and silliness. Most of the activities were dependent on the co-operation of the whole group, which meant that just one child could interrupt the smooth flow of the lesson. However, in general this factor encouraged everyone to participate, with fellow students often encouraging others to co-operate and listen, in order to play the game. This group dynamic led to many positive group experiences of shared attention and enjoyment.

One critical aspect of the programme was the decision to spend the first few weeks consolidating very basic rhythm skills, from which further musical skills could later develop. Thus, rhythmic clapping games took immediate priority, followed by singing games and then the introduction of percussion instruments and more complex rhythm games. Towards the end of the programme, chime bars were also introduced. Since the programme was intended for classroom use, none of the games involved running or dancing, but the philosophy of play from ETM was retained to as great an extent as possible. Examples of some rhythm games and how they were conducted are described below.

Examples of rhythm games

The following selection of rhythm games draws particularly on activities and ideas from *Earwiggo Again – Rhythm Games* (West and Holdstock, 1985), as discussed above.

The Name Game

It is always fun to begin group work with name games, since children usually like to say their own name and to have others focus on their name. Names are also useful because they are over-familiar and are thus a good starting point for identifying the natural 'rhythm' of the words (that is the segmentation of the syllables).

In this game, the children sit in a circle and the leader begins a rhythmic pattern, which the children copy. The pattern consists of a steady beat with actions: two claps followed by dropping the hands on the knees and holding for a beat (Figure 4.1 below).

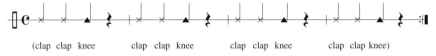

(clap clap knee)   clap clap knee   clap clap knee   clap clap knee)

Figure 4.1. The Name Game clapping pattern.

Once the pattern is going comfortably and steadily, without speeding up, the leader explains that everyone is going to say their own name in the gaps, going around the circle. The leader then begins and the children copy (Figure 4.2).

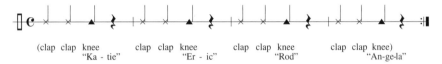

(clap clap knee   clap clap knee   clap clap knee   clap clap knee)
"Ka - tie"   "Er - ic"   "Rod"   "An-ge-la"

Figure 4.2. The Name Game word pattern.

Some children may have difficulties at first trying to co-ordinate their hand movements with their speech, and they may muddle up the clap-knee sequence, or say their name at the wrong time. This is always treated as fun and a game and never as a mistake. The rest of the children are encouraged to keep the beat going and not be distracted by one child getting muddled up. The children are also encouraged to take their time and are allowed to wait for a pattern or two to go by before they say their name, in order to concentrate fully. If children say their name without the correct rhythm, the leader can wait until the circle has been completed and then focus on a couple of names (still keeping the rhythm pattern going) and have everyone say them rhythmically together.

Once the children are reasonably confident at saying their own names at the correct moment, the leader can move on to other choices of words, such as 'surnames', 'colours', 'drinks' and so forth. Ideally, the rhythmic pattern should be continuous and the leader should simply suggest a new category each time the circle is completed, to which the children must immediately respond (for example 'coke', 'lemonade', 'orange juice', 'gin'). This adds a huge element of fun and tension to the game, as the children try to think of what word they are going to say, as it gets closer to their turn. The focus inevitably moves to the humour and interest in the choice of words, while the process of learning to keep a steady beat while co-ordinating physical actions and while speaking words rhythmically goes almost unnoticed. There is an excellent opportunity here for children to have fun and think creatively, and, as their skills improve, the tempo of the beat can get faster and faster.

Figure 4.3. Pass the Beater.

Pass the Beater

This melody is very easy to pick up, and the words are just about impossible to forget (Figure 4.3). The game also involves useful physical actions for practising both metre and rhythm skills.

The children sit on the floor in a circle, with a drum (or woodblock or something similar) in the centre. The beater for the drum can be just about anything but is preferably wooden, to make a pleasant sound as it hits the floor during the song. The leader begins by singing the song and firmly placing a beater on the floor in front of the child to the left, the first time the word 'pass' is uttered. The children are then encouraged to continue to pass the beater in time with the music by placing the beater in front of the person to their left exactly on the word 'pass'. The word 'pass' helps the children to focus on making sure the beater hits the floor at exactly the right time, which demands good listening (in order to stay in time with everyone else) and good motor co-ordination. The resulting percussive accompaniment to the song (caused by the beater hitting the floor) emphasises the first beat of each bar.

When the song ends, the child who is left holding the beater is invited into the centre of the circle to play the drum. The leader claps individual rhythms and the child copies. This is a fun way to practise listening and rhythm copying, since most children are desperate to have a turn and to stay for as long as possible in the centre. The teacher can begin with very simple rhythms and lead up to more complicated ones, depending on the skills of the child. If an error is made, the leader can simply repeat the same rhythm again and again, until the child gets it correct, with no need to even comment on whether it was wrong or right. The other children in the circle are also encouraged to listen carefully (but not to comment: only the person in the middle can make a sound).

An advantage of this song game is that the emphasis lies on passing the beater correctly and on who will get the beater; so the children are happy to sing, without feeling as self-conscious as they might in other circumstances. From time to time, the leader can ask the children to sing quietly, slowly, loudly, sadly, scarily and so forth. And, of course, as the children get better at the game, the tempo can increase.

Spot the Difference

This is a simple game that can be played quietly in a circle. To begin with, the leader simply claps a number of beats and the number is passed around the circle until it gets back to the leader. The leader then changes the number of beats and the number is passed around the circle again. The leader then selects a child to be the person to change the number of beats and the process continues. When everyone is able to perform the skills of copying and changing the number of beats (not necessarily easy for everyone), one child is asked to leave the room and the leader selects another child to be the person to change the number of beats. The first child then re-enters the room and attempts to spot which person is making the change, while a number is passed around the circle. The focus of the game turns very quickly to the fun of choosing who will leave the room and then spotting who has changed the beat; the children do not notice that they are having to concentrate on their fine-motor skills and listening skills.

This game can be kept very simple by limiting the number of beats to three or four and keeping the tempo very steady. Alternatively, the game can be made more difficult by allowing any number of beats (within reason) and gradually increasing the tempo. In general, mistakes will be made through attempts to be too fast, which are funny and not in any way wrong. A more advanced version of the game is to use rhythms instead of numbers, which involves particularly good listening skills, as well as rhythm copying and rhythm discrimination skills. For example, rhythm A (Figure 4.4) might be passed around the circle and then changed to rhythm B (Figure 4.5).

Figure 4.4. Rhythm A.

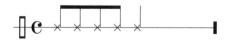

Figure 4.5. Rhythm B.

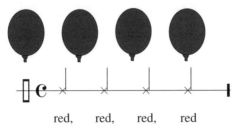

red,   red,   red,   red

Figure 4.6. Red Balloons.

Rhythm Balloons

This idea can be used to lead children slowly into musical literacy. Four red cut-out paper balloons (in the following figures, the red balloons are black and the yellow balloons are light grey) are placed on the floor in front of the children and the leader demonstrates how to tap a steady beat to the words 'red, red, red, red' (Figure 4.6).

The leader then points at the balloons in time, while the children follow with their percussion instruments (or clapping or chime bars). When the group is able to keep a steady beat going, without speeding up (not that easy), the leader adds four yellow balloons to the red balloons and demonstrates how to change the rhythm pattern for the yellows (Figure 4.7).

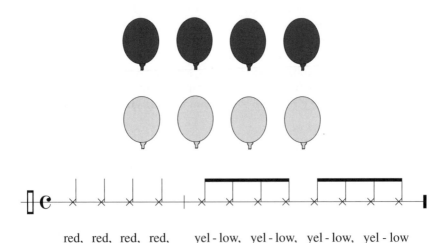

red, red, red, red,   yel - low, yel - low, yel - low, yel - low

Figure 4.7. Red and Yellow Balloons.

Figure 4.8. Mixed Red and Yellow Balloons.

The children then follow on their percussion instruments, as the leader points to the balloons. The pointing helps to emphasise the practice of reading music from left to right and also helps to keep the children in time and together. The grouping of four balloons per line helps to establish the musical feeling of four beats in a bar. When the children are comfortable with the rhythmic difference between red and yellow and are able to keep a steady beat going, the leader moves some of the balloons around to create a new pattern. For example, see Figure 4.8.

This can be performed by the leader first, followed by the whole group and then by soloists (each on a different percussion instrument, which varies the sound quality). The activity can continue with a variety of different combinations of red and yellow balloons, becoming as complex as possible. Extra balloons can lead to further combinations and children can compose their own rhythms by arranging their own patterns of balloons, which can be shared with the whole group. In time, the balloons can also be turned over, revealing a white underneath to indicate a rest. Additional lines of balloons can also be included, creating longer rhythms, and a variety of games can be played, with soloists, duets or with two groups with different rhythms, for example. It is fun even just to have one group of instruments playing simply reds, while another group plays yellows. This requires very good listening and motor co-ordination skills. Another game is for the children to create a number of lines of balloons and for the leader to perform the rhythm, stopping at a random point. The children have to keep track and point to the balloon at which the leader stopped. There is, in fact, no end to the potential activities, all of which are reinforcing the simple sounds of crotchets, quavers and rests, within simple rhythmic patterns.

Rhythm Squares

For this activity, a cardboard square is divided into 16 smaller squares and the children fill each small square with a red or yellow dot of their own choice (Figure 4.9).

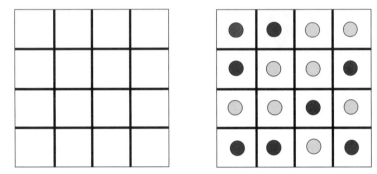

Figure 4.9. Rhythm Squares.

The rhythm square can then be 'performed' in much the same way as the rhythm balloons are 'performed', either by the whole class or by individuals or groups. The squares can also be turned around and upside down, to create different rhythm patterns. Children enjoy having their own rhythm square performed by the rest of the group and perhaps then turned upside down and performed again. Games can be created using different musical instruments, different groups of children performing different colours, different lines and so forth.

One particular advantage of the rhythm square is that the children can start to see, hear and feel some of the regular phrasing patterns in music. For example, a simple rhythmic pattern is shown in Figure 4.10 below.

The 'same, same, different, same' (or AABA) structure of this rhythm square is very typical of a great deal of folk, pop and classical music and helps the listener to become particularly aware of the 'different' section. The visual pattern of the rhythm square emphasises the relationships between the different sections, heightening both auditory and kinaesthetic awareness of the regularities and irregularities.

Another advantage of the rhythm square is that different individuals or groups of children can perform different rhythm squares at the same time, leading to more complicated rhythmic textures. It takes a great deal of concentration and focused attention for two groups of children to perform two different rhythm squares together successfully. Both groups must be able to feel the beat very comfortably and must listen carefully to

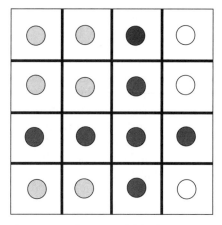

Figure 4.10. Structured Rhythm Square.

the combined sound texture in order to stay in time. The results are very rewarding though and there is a great deal of opportunity for the children and the leader to be creative in different ways. The activities also pave the way for musical literacy, beginning with black dots and bar lines and moving on as appropriate.

Discussion

The games described above focus entirely on rhythm skills and represent only some of the games in the musical activities programme but, nevertheless, give a good representation of the type of musical engagement that was encouraged. Overall, the procedure and specific content of the music lessons was quite variable, regularly adapting in accordance with the changing needs and requests of the children. For example, in one lesson we ended up creating a rap version of *April Showers* (from the 1921 Broadway musical *Bombo*) and in another we all sang, stamped and clapped along with Queen's *We Will Rock You* (1977).

Thus, the activities programme described above is in many respects a work in progress, with future classroom use required to develop and refine it. The programme is currently being used in two primary schools in London, and the teacher involved has gradually selected preferred games, added new games and identified the fact that three music sessions per week seem to be crucial for good continuity and successful learning.

Significant improvements in phonological skills have been reported so far, with some cases of improved literacy skills.

In the original intervention study conducted as part of my PhD research, the musical activities were conducted three times a week for 20 to 30 minutes at a time, for 15 weeks. The results of music, language and literacy tests showed that, compared to a 15-week period with no musical intervention (just school visits from me, with individual reading time), the children improved significantly in their rhythm skills, phonological skills and spelling skills. This demonstrated for the first time that rhythm-based music lessons can help dyslexic children, and led to the development of a new theoretical model of the way in which musical experience can influence language skills (Overy, 2003), recently developed further in the journal *Trends in Neurosciences* (Tallal and Gaab, 2006), as discussed in Chapter 19. However, the study was extremely small-scale and so further studies involving larger numbers of children of various age groups, and with control interventions, will be necessary to support these findings.

Of course, a particular advantage of the musical activities programme is the fact that, regardless of academic outcomes, there is an emphasis on enjoyment, fun and musical learning. Genuine interest and enjoyment are the strongest motivation for children to concentrate and lead to the greatest development in skills. Positive experiences also take the focus away from any difficulties children might be encountering at school. The programme is also very flexible, since it was designed to be adaptable to the skills and needs of different children in different circumstances, rather than requiring the children to conform to and achieve pre-determined procedures and tasks. This flexibility is particularly important for dyslexic children, whose skills vary considerably not only between children but also from day to day.

Another important aspect of the music programme is the fact that its design was based on a combination of theory, research and practice. The three music education methods described above were selected very carefully: they were designed specifically for use with groups of young children with the general aim of engaging all children in music and not just the most talented. The method most drawn on for the music programme was *Earwiggo*, which was created by people with a wealth of experience with children with learning difficulties. The programme was also significantly influenced pedagogically and methodologically by both *Growing with Music* and Education Through Music, which were also designed by people with many years of teaching experience. In addition, both of the latter methods are based on the Kodály approach to music education, which was developed very thoroughly over many decades throughout the national education system in Hungary. Furthermore, the Kodály approach itself was the result of research into the best music education methods in Europe at the beginning of the twentieth century.

The musical activities programme is thus based on very strong foundations, while also benefiting enormously from the practical process of working with dyslexic children, which has led to a number of adaptations and developments. It is hoped that this programme will continue to be used, developed and evaluated, with the help of musicians, classroom teachers and educational psychologists.

References

Blythe, S. (1998) Music Matters. *Music Teacher* **September**: 43.

Chan, A.S., Ho, Y-C. and Cheung, M-C. (1998) Music training improves verbal memory. *Nature* **396**(12 November): 128.

Goswami, U., Thomson, J., Richardson, U., Stainthorp, R. *et al.* (2002) Amplitude envelope onsets and developmental dyslexia: a new hypothesis. *Proceedings of the National Academy of Sciences of the United States of America* **99**(16): 10911–10916.

Habib, M., Rey, V., Daffaure, V., Camps, R. *et al.* (2002) Phonological training in children with dyslexia using temporally modified speech: a three-step pilot investigation. *International Journal of Communication Disorders* **37**(3): 289–308.

Hurwitz, I., Wolff, P., Bortnick, B. and Kokas, K. (1975) Non-musical effects of the Kodály music curriculum in primary grade children. *Journal of Learning Disabilities* **8**(3): 45–52.

Johansen, K.V. (2000) Hearing, Central Auditory Processing Disorders and Reading Problems. Paper presented at the International Dyslexia Association 51st Annual Conference, Washington, DC, 8–11 November.

Kolb, G.R. (1996) Read with a beat: developing literacy through music and song. *The Reading Teacher* **50**(1): 76–77.

MacLean, M., Bryant, P.E. and Bradley, L. (1987) Rhymes, nursery rhymes and reading in early childhood. *Merrill-Palmer Quarterly* **33**(3): 255–281.

Nicolson, R.I., Fawcett, A.J. and Dean, P. (1995) Time estimation deficits in developmental dyslexia: evidence for cerebellar involvement. *Proceedings of the Royal Society: Biological Society* **259**(1354): 43–47.

O'Connor, R.E., Notarie-Syverson, A. and Vadasy, P.F. (1998) *Ladders to Literacy: A Kindergarten Activity Book.* Paul H. Brookes Publishing Co., Baltimore.

Oglethorpe, S. (1996) *Instrumental Music for Dyslexics: A Teaching Handbook.* Whurr, London.

Overy K. (2003) Dyslexia and music from timing deficits to musical intervention. *Annals of the New York Academy of Sciences* **999**: 497–505.

Overy, K. (2002) *Dyslexia and Music: From Timing Deficits to Music Intervention.* PhD Thesis. University of Sheffield, UK.

Overy, K. (1997) *Music, Mental Skills and Education.* MA Dissertation, University of Sheffield, UK.

Overy, K., Nicolson, R.I., Fawcett, A.J. and Clarke, E.F. (2003) Dyslexia and music: measuring musical timing skills. *Dyslexia* 9(1): 18–36.

Richards, M.H. (1977) *Aesthetic Foundations for Thinking.* Richards Institute of Music Education and Research, California.

Slevc, L.R. and Miyake, A. (2006) Individual differences in second-language proficiency: does musical ability matter? *Psychological Science* **17**(8): 675–681.

Stocks, M. and Maddocks, A. (1992) *Growing with Music.* Longman Group, Harlow, Essex.

Sutton, J. (1995) The sound-world of speech- and language-impaired children: the story of a current music therapy research project. In A. Gilroy (ed), *Art and Music, Therapy and Research*, Routledge, London.

Tallal, P. and Gaab, N. (2006) Dynamic auditory processing, musical experience and language development. *Trends in Neurosciences* **29**(7): 382–90.

Tallal, P., Miller, S. and Fitch, R.H. (1993) Neurobiological basis of speech: a case for the pre-eminence of temporal processing. *Annals of the New York Academy of Sciences* **682**(14 June): 27–47.

Trevarthen, C. (1999) Musicality and the intrinsic motive pulse: evidence from human psychobiology and infant communication. *Musicae Scientiae* (Special Issue 1999/2000, Rhythms, musical narrative, and the origins of human communication): 157–213.

West, L. and Holdstock, J. (1985) *Earwiggo Again – Rhythm Games.* Yorkshire and Humberside Association for Music in Special Education.

West, L. and Holdstock, J. (1984) *Earwiggo – Listening Games.* Yorkshire and Humberside Association for Music in Special Education.

Wolf, M. and Bowers, P. (2000) The question of naming-speed deficits in developmental reading disability: an introduction to the Double-Deficit Hypothesis. *Journal of Learning Disabilities* **33**: 322–324.

five

Early years: Deirdre starts to learn piano

Olivia McCarthy and Diana Ditchfield

Deirdre was assessed as being dyslexic when she was 7.6 years and received targeted academic extra-curricular teaching for her particular pattern of dyslexia until she was about 14 years old. After this, she was heartily sick of all this extra work and of being 'different' and put her foot down and refused any more of it. Nevertheless, by this time she was happily settled in secondary school, where she was doing very well. She has since taken her Leaving Certificate and has started studying at university to do an arts degree.

Nevertheless, at the age of 5 and during her first year at primary school Deirdre's problems were serious. Although she attended an excellent school close to her home and was raised in comfortable, happy and supportive circumstances, she was so disruptive that the school was very reluctant to allow her to remain and proceed to the second year. Eventually, because her older brother, who attended the same school, was a clever child and the family were good supporters of the school, Deirdre was kept on. Her mother later explained to Diana that even though she had sat beside the same girl at the shared desk for the whole of the school year she was unable to remember the girl's name at the end of the year.

It was during this year that Olivia taught Deirdre piano at the local school of music where she and Diana both teach piano. Diana's experiences, which have been recorded in *Music and Dyslexia: Opening New Doors* (Ditchfield, 2001), followed Olivia's when the timetable assigned Deirdre to Diana rather than Olivia. The observations and teaching/learning experiences with Deirdre in this chapter took place during her first year of learning piano. It is hoped they will inform and assist those who encounter unusual and unexpected challenges in teaching piano to very young children. It also supports the value of structured, cumulative, individually targeted multisensory teaching, both for the dyslexic and non-dyslexic alike. What is good for the dyslexic is likely also to be good for the non-dyslexic. While being conversant with the methodology associated with Dalcroze and Kodály and others, we draw on all of the teaching and learning resources that may be utilised in an interactional interpersonal situation as they seem appropriate, without slavishly following any particular named method.

When Deirdre was presented for enrolment into the music school where Diana and Olivia teach, her older brother was also enrolled as a new piano student with a different teacher at the same time, and there was a younger sister at home. There would be sibling comparisons and all involved knew that, by virtue of the age difference, the older child who had already acquired some literacy would progress more quickly. A one-to-one situation permits a personal and immediate response. There are guideline curricular norms in the school which tend to define success or failure, although, at the age of 5, progress is often uneven and erratic, with varying difficulties and/or abilities expected for all children.

Deirdre always seemed surprised when she opened her music case and found all of her music books and the class diary there; they were never returned to her music case in the tidy fashion in which they had been extracted! The lesson time, straight after school, suggested Deirdre would be tired and the requirement to concentrate at this time would be demanding of any child. However, it was not long before it was observed that levels of concentration, retention and attention were different and below average compared with other children of the same age whom Diana taught. Deirdre appeared to concentrate intensely for short periods of time, and this seemed to exclude her use of other cues/senses; she focused on the notes until 'shut down'; she looked intently at the page, which puzzled her so much that it seemed she was unable to get any clues from her other senses as to what it was all about. Freedom of physical response seemed hindered by visual concerns and worries, and by the end of the first term Deirdre was not able to confidently play any notated piece of music she had been studying; she was not at ease with any page in the book.

Good teaching requires avoiding the point of 'shut down', but this was very difficult, as Deirdre seemed to be overwhelmed by information very quickly. Beginning and ending each lesson optimistically and successfully, therefore, was also not easy. There was no safe territory or favourite piece or activity. It transpired from a later assessment for specific learning difficulty (dyslexia) that a deficient short-term memory was one of Deirdre's chief problems.

Deirdre's seating and hand positions were not a problem, which was a very positive achievement on Deirdre's part. There also appeared to be a good understanding of the relationship between physical action and dynamic level, and Deirdre was able to produce the sound she sought. This suggested also that there was aural awareness; she seemed surprised by sudden changes of dynamics. The later dyslexia assessment noted no problems with gross- or fine-motor co-ordination, or with sound discrimination or sound blending. However, in primary school, Deirdre had great difficulty with phonics and phonological processing. It is now believed that musical and phonological sounds are heard and processed differently by the ears and in the brain.

A very noticeable difference with Deirdre in comparison with other children at the same age and stage was her sense of rhythm. She did not seem familiar with well-known nursery rhymes and did not seem to have the usual pleasure from clapping and marching games. Deirdre appeared to have very varying responses to these, which made it difficult to build complexity. It has now been established that there is a strong relationship between rhythm and reading and that, although weak rhythm at this age is not a safe determinant of dyslexia, nevertheless, it is a possible indicator. This raises the interesting question as to whether rhythmic exercises during music lessons could conceivably be useful remedial exercises in assisting dyslexics with literacy (see Chapter 4).

The acquisition of musical notational literacy was below average and revision in note reading was almost a new exercise each time it was carried out; we all forget things. However, Deirdre appeared unable to grasp the concept of the aural/visual relationship between the clefs and was unable to bring into play the use of aural/tactile senses to fill in the gaps, as would often be the case with a child of similar age. In addition, Deirdre's confusion with the printed page seemed to be preventing her from developing other musical skills, and also her fear of failure was taking up too much concentration and prevented her from focusing on her successes. Generally, a child of this age is more likely to misread than mishear, but a combination of reading and hearing often allows a child to self-correct. At this stage, Deirdre was unable to combine these two senses in learning to play the piano, and it was a challenge to the teacher to prevent discouragement. Frequent changes of activity helped, but too many of these can simply add confusion.

When reading pitch, Deirdre appeared to have no alternative strategy in place. For example, familiarity with other features on the page would, for other children, prompt their musical memory and performance, but Deirdre's attention immediately focused intently on the actual notation. This difficulty with gaining an overview and relating all features on the page together therefore delayed the acquisition of musical terminology where instructions regarding tempo or dynamics, for example, were transferred from pictures to words.

Musical progress should not be limited by reading ability. Melodic memory, rhythmic memory, muscular memory and aural memory may be developed by rote learning, especially if supported in a paired situation, with the teacher singing, playing or clapping/tapping. Greater security and confidence, as well as a sense of success and enjoyment, are gained in this way, and this teaching strategy was employed to good effect. As dyslexics are very familiar with failing, it is essential that self-confidence is fostered at all possible opportunities.

In this first year, Deirdre did not interact with her music book. For example, at this stage, she did not personalise her music books with colourings and drawings, although she was happy to draw in her manuscript book or notebook or on the window. Very basic forms of graphic notation were introduced and there was a frequent switching of focus from the task in hand to an external action, such as a toy figure walking across the lid of the piano. Unlike most children, Deirdre had no interest in repeating any action, for example in playing a piece twice. Although the pattern of the lesson tends to have a familiar order, there was no sense of anticipation. A sense of time elapsed or sequential activities are often acquired much later by the dyslexic compared with the non-dyslexic. Deirdre did not appear to gain any sense of assurance or comfort from routine. It was a challenge to the teacher to retain Deirdre's attention and enjoyment during her half-hour lesson, mindful at all times that it was a piano lesson and she wished to foster and develop a sense of musical enjoyment and ability in Deirdre. Teaching in the music lesson was not confined to sitting at the piano. Where Deirdre enjoyed walking round the room 'plinking' the piano, it was used for aural development – as was listening to music. However, the latter activity always had to involve Deirdre in doing something, as she was quite unable to sit quietly and listen for any length of time.

While flexibility is important, it is also important to have some targets for the term and the year which are (a) achievable, (b) hopeful and likely, and also (c) improbable but not impossible (as it is important for the child, parent and teacher to have a tangible result in a defined period of time). Thus, thought was re-focused on the primary and secondary aims of the lessons. These were defined as (a) learning to play the piano, (b) reading music, (c) developing musical sensibility and musicianship, (d) responding to music and (e) training in eye–hand co-ordination.

Every teacher has a personalised style. Suffice it to say, Deirdre enjoyed her lessons sufficiently to be keen to continue the following year, even after a long summer holiday. Indeed, she continued learning piano up until she entered secondary school, when the pressure of work and the additional time spent with academic extra-curricular tuition demanded some rationalisation. Deirdre's parents endeavoured to allow her to be exposed to all manner of stimuli and she attended dance, elocution and gymnastics classes after school on a regular basis. She became socially well adjusted with many friends amongst her peers. She enjoyed singing at secondary school and took part in school musical productions, although she did not continue to learn piano or take up any other musical instrument.

It is difficult to quantify the value of early learning of a musical instrument for either a dyslexic or non-dyslexic child. Research in Canada (Trainor and Fujioka, 2006) suggests that early musical training has a beneficial effect on IQ and memory. It is, however, a great encouragement in this longitudinal study to note that Deirdre has developed normally, and with a sense of personal well-being. Indicators of differences and imbalances were clearly visible in early piano lessons, and these differences had already been noted by Deirdre's mother, even before she attended primary school or piano lessons. Augur (1990) asks the question, 'Is three too young to know?' and suggests that early indicators of dyslexia are noticed by some who are close to young dyslexics and familiar with some of problems associated with the syndrome. In Deirdre's case, these were later confirmed as being visual-perceptual (sequential and spatial), short-term-memory, organisational, phonological, concentration and attention problems, and with an added degree of hyperactivity. Her strengths were auditory and motor, with added degrees of intelligence and family support. However, in a climate in which 'dyslexia' was not a household word, her mother did not initially know what caused them. She, alongside other diligent and caring teachers, employed all her skills with openness and kindness in helping Deirdre, and it is a credit to all, including the very hard work and persistence of Deirdre herself, that she has achieved so much at this stage of her life.

The value of learning to play the piano as a diagnostic and remedial tool

Although it would be invidious to regard music and learning to play the piano as simply a tool to address various difficulties associated with dyslexia, nevertheless there may be collateral benefits which can help in the assessment and/or remediation of dyslexia. While being mindful of individual differences in general, an experienced piano teacher can sometimes notice difficulties associated with dyslexia. Music is a comprehensive discipline involving all the domains of intelligence, and strengths and weaknesses may be evident. These weaknesses may be identified as numerical, sequential (auditory and visual) or organisational or to do with aspects of motor, concentration or retention skills, or understood in terms of sensibility or other personal attitudes such as application, perseverance, motivation – or any combination of any of these.

A musical instrument is generally taught on a one-to-one basis. This allows for individual assessment and supported, structured and cumulative progress in a dynamic and creative manner. Teaching may be both adjusted to the learner's existing learning styles and may also be used to approach unfamiliar or unwelcome learning which may be either essential or beneficial for the purpose in hand. Some examples are suggested below.

A child may have difficulty with the mathematical aspects of time and rhythm. Many approaches to this problem are suggested by Oglethorpe (1996). Music may be reduced to two beats in a bar *if* this suits a child better than understanding four beats. Tapping by hand, watching, listening, touching and sensing a vibrating regular beat through the hands and maybe tapping the foot alongside can help with understanding and reproducing rhythm and time, as can playing with the teacher. Dyslexic children sometimes have difficulty with walking or marching in time with music which has a regular beat. There is an element of multisensory training which can be used both to acquire the specific skill sought and transfer the learning from it, or from acquiring it, into other areas of learning. Moreover, it is worth remembering that the acquisition of the actual skill may precede the understanding of the content or process of what has been learnt. The resources of music are enormous and may be utilised dynamically by an experienced and sensitive piano teacher.

The size and strength of the hand, fingers and the body develop as the child grows. These aspects should be accommodated, employed and developed in the service of learning the piano, without over-extension. The physical requirement to assimilate the space, for example between the notes on the keyboard of E and F sharp, eventually becomes physically automatic; this physical ability may then be transferred to a theoretical understanding of key, for example, and this skill may be utilised in a different setting – or the process could occur in reverse for some children.

Concentration may be improved not just by individually supported learning but also especially by sharing enjoyment of music with the child so that motivation is also fostered and encouraged.

The absence of words and phonics is often a great relief to the dyslexic child, although it is inevitable that words will increasingly become part of the picture at some point, hopefully when there is sufficient confidence for them to be accepted without too much difficulty. Constant revision and rehearsal are required in learning a musical instrument, and, apart from physical aspects, this notional skill is also transferable into other areas of learning. 'Practice makes Perfect' is more than simply learning to play the piano!

When written theory is being learnt, a child's motor skills are employed differently as they need to write with a pencil; some children find it very difficult to put a semibreve on bottom line treble clef E without it appearing to be bottom space treble clef F. There are specific orders and patterns which are constantly repeated in music and, once these are rehearsed ritually, this familiarity and confidence in patterns and order is reassuring for a dyslexic child. Notational aspects of the horizontal and vertical have to be employed and this may present difficulties. The teacher will need to be creative in helping these spatial aspects to be taken on board. Patience is also required as the actual point of understanding for the child occurs when the child is ready and able to understand. All these aspects are transferable into other areas of learning and the advantage is that learning the piano uses multisensory means at all times.

Music progresses, both on the page and in the heard sounds. Sometimes the concept of time elapsed is a problem for the dyslexic child and the learning of eight progressive bars of music helps remediate the difficulty. If the child is able to vocalise by singing the tune, or even putting letters or fingering to the tune (maybe a scale), this can reinforce learning in a cumulative multisensory manner.

Visualisation is to be encouraged. Some children can play scales or other music simply by the visualisation of the music on the keyboard in a geographical manner, which is supported by the sound of the music and the discrimination of whether the sound is 'correct'.

Great support is sometimes required to move from the familiar to the unfamiliar. The teacher can sensitively reassure and foster this requirement and also, thereby, help set a pattern for the future where new things are welcome or even sought and are no longer frightening or 'impossible'. We all enjoy employing either innate or learnt skills and these may become tools we can manipulate for our own use and pleasure. In terms of playing the piano, this is sometimes referred to as 'technique'.

Apart from the techniques learnt, there are aspects of sensibility.

Margaret Donaldson (1987) refers to the close relationship between the growth of consciousness and the growth of the intellect, and it is reasonable to argue that learning to play the piano may also feed into this process.

Organisational difficulties are sometimes associated with dyslexia, and the requirement to be highly organised when learning and playing the piano can be supported and become a useful skill. It may be that the parents/guardians of the child are glad of some assistance with helping their charges.

It is difficult to quantify the benefits of learning to play a musical instrument in addressing the diagnosis and remediation of the difficulties of dyslexia, not least because the growing child is absorbing and processing many different types of information. Music should above all be a pleasurable experience and the aspects discussed above should always remain subsidiary.

References

Augur J (1990) Is three too young to know? *Dyslexia Contact* 9(1): 10–11.

Ditchfield, D. (2001) Teaching the piano to Deidre. In: *Music and Dyslexia: Opening New Doors*, T.R. Miles and J. Westcombe (eds), Whurr, London.

Donaldson, M. (1987) *Children's Minds*, Fontana Press, London.

Oglethorpe, S. (1996) *Instrumental Music for Dyslexics: A Teaching Handbook*, Whurr, London.

Trainor, L. and Fujioka, T. (2006) First evidence that musical training affects brain development in young children, http://www.sciencedaily.com/releases/2006/09/060920093024.htm, accessed 1 August 2007.

Cameo Two

Some thoughts about early years

Pauline Poole, John Westcombe and Diana Ditchfield

Pauline Poole introduces this cameo

I believe in music in early years as creative fun, an indicator of special learning difficulties (SpLDs) and remedial support for pre-literary experiences. In some cases, music is a great vehicle for learning in early years and also the 'big spike' to balance the lows caused by

SpLD problems. As a teenager, however, it is also an outlet for the dyslexic's frustrations!

My son Mark's difficulties with notation led him to change from violin to drums. We had decided that the theory side would prove frustrating in GCSE, and chose to do electronics instead. His music teacher petitioned us from April to July, claiming that Mark was a gifted musician he (the staff member) was anxious to have in the examination class. The change was made and he is thoroughly enjoying the course, although I remain concerned about the examination requirements. His drum lessons are going well and he plays the drums at church.

Now John Westcombe and Diana Ditchfield join with Pauline to expand on this theme below.

Blues in the early years

Many children have very early experiences in music and respond in different ways. Some have greater difficulty than their peers in remembering nursery rhymes, learning tunes and articulating lyrics or get them jumbled up – difficulties that may indicate an SpLD and can be early-warning signs for an alert practitioner. On the other hand, some have outstanding early gifts in hearing and repeating a tune, moving and keeping the beat. These should be logged as they may form part of the 'spiky profile' of a dyslexic individual, as mentioned above.

For all children, music can be enjoyable and satisfy creative needs. It can also provide invaluable support – for remediating weakness in hearing rhyme and rhythm, speech development and learning sequences – which can ameliorate early literacy learning.

Some early developmental situations will be glimpsed and 'partnered' with some 'differences seen', usually by a mother. These differences are often identified as being 'different from peers', even if it is her first child. Carefully exposing the infant to multiple stimuli can assist overall healthy development. Alongside this, the view that screening should be done earlier than hitherto is gaining much support. In any event, by the end of Key Stage 2, many differences will have fallen into place within the overall development and emerging personality of the young person. However, some will remain, and it is essential to identify and allow attention to these so as to give maximum encouragement.

Is there a difference between helping the dyslexics with their music and using music to help their dyslexia? In so far as they require different expertise, the answer has to be 'yes'.

Many children show a physical response to music, for example in dance and movement. Some can pitch and sing in tune and follow a beat; some march to strong Common Time music; some can dance a polka, hornpipe, jig and so on. Although it is not always the case, generally the dyslexic has more difficulty with these aspects than his or her counterpart. Further, the dyslexic will be perplexed when presented with musical notation. It can be a fraught situation and requires patience and as much expertise as can be mustered in terms of keeping the child on board and making positive progress. There then follows the problem of co-ordinating the reading of musical notation and getting it along the main pathways through the brain to the hands, voice or feet, and reproducing it as music on the flute or in dancing or singing. These can be trying, if illuminating, times for the non-dyslexic and often magnified for the dyslexic child.

Singing is a great help in assisting in the breaking down of words into their syllables, thus aiding the critical phonological element.

The dyslexic child will be helped by practice in rhythm, nursery rhymes, games etc., particularly any material which has a call and answer structure. (See Chapter 4.) Working in these activities is not beyond the good teaching instincts and reactions of the class teacher. Many teachers are far too modest in these matters – they don't have to be trained musicians to have a teacherly view of how a piece being composed by a group might take alternative paths.

So, the dyslexic young person can be helped to read by musical activities; their musical counterpart will probably need help to improve their music once the staves and symbols make their appearance.

six

Winning over the reluctants

Christine McRitchie Pratt, Diana Ditchfield, Sheila Oglethorpe and John Westcombe

Individual music making should be rewarding and enjoyable. Particular care needs to be taken to ensure that a person with traits of dyslexia is well supervised.

Any lack of enthusiasm for music might arise for several reasons. Sensitive discussions need to take place about styles of teaching, just as much as of learning. Is there ever discussion about whether the approach the teacher takes is that to which the pupil responds best? Pupils and parents need to be aware of all possible factors which might prevent an easy progression, as most young people like to feel that they are getting on, but some don't like to be too pressured or tied to Grade examinations. Pupils must feel comfortable with the instrument they are learning, the timing of lessons and surroundings. Schools can sometimes be inhospitable places at the beginning and end of the day. At home, sitting on the most comfortable chair in the room where practice is done may well induce bad posture, and a properly firm music stand is critical.

Lately, there has been an encouraging commitment from the Government to extend access to instruments through LEAs and schools. This is welcome, long overdue and should bring many more opportunities for pupils to experience all kinds of instruments. Further, by this and other methods, pupils can see that by no means all music is notation-bound. The great bodies of jazz, improvisation and music from other continents are not. And so, just because music is not recorded on the page does not mean that it cannot be played or sung.

Dyslexics often prefer to learn a piece from memory, to discern what it sounds like before seeing what it looks like, and this can include the teacher playing it for them.

Exactly what helps pupils (including adults) to look forward to lessons and the practice which attends them? We know a young lady who anticipates the enjoyment of lessons partly because she enjoys meeting the teacher's dog and cat. More seriously, there needs to be a sense of progress, creating and performing with others, of being able to show the results of work between lessons, as well as the discovery of new repertoire.

There may be reluctants who ought to be in the groups that the school organises. Sometimes it is almost an external thing – like going to an attractive concert or meeting a charismatic, professional, visiting musician who sets the individual towards involvement. This sometimes happens when teachers and parents have offered all sorts of other blandishments, apparently without response – disturbing! Availability and choice of instruments are critical, and we have to understand that the instrument which a young person may choose may not be the one all earlier signs have pointed to, or the one parents would have most liked.

Should we worry if the young person decides that an electronic keyboard is a more congenial starter instrument than the piano?

If it happens that the learner is dyslexic, and has known that they are for some time, it is particularly important to understand the major cause of reluctance. It may simply be not liking the current pieces, finding a particular passage troublesome or getting round the 'it looks like sight-reading every time I look at it' situation. Here, a brick-by-brick, multisensory, structured programme initiated by the teacher (which uses minimal practice notes and writing and focuses more on the practical, non-reading aspects of music learning), buttressed by the thoughtful support of parents or carers, is so important. Is it just the mechanics of reading off the page that's the trouble – have eyes been tested recently? Have coloured transparencies been tried? Has the pupil recently transferred to the secondary sector? And are there just too many activities to try to be in?

Participating in music holds possibilities of infinite pleasure, and parents, carers and teachers need to listen carefully to a young person for whom this appears not to be true.

The basis of this short chapter appeared originally in the British Dyslexia Association's journal Contact **24**(2), *in May of 2005. The editors are grateful for permission to use it.*

seven

Can music lessons help the dyslexic learner?

Sheila Oglethorpe

Introduction

The question 'Can music lessons help the dyslexic learner?' is often asked. It is possible to answer it in several different ways, according to what the questioner really means. They may mean: 'If a dyslexic is learning to read music, does it make them better at reading words or even at doing mental arithmetic?' I suspect that sometimes the questioner is rather vague about what they mean, but perhaps they are hoping that music, in some way, can be the answer to a multiplicity of difficulties that a dyslexic may have, ranging from a poor short-term memory and perhaps organisational and sequencing problems to bizarre spelling and an apparent reading block that won't go away.

'Music' today is a term with very fuzzy edges, and it is perhaps unwise to restrict it to the sort of traditional classical sounds that, for the last eight centuries or more, until, perhaps, the beginning of the twenty-first century, have been handed down to us in the Western world. However, in view of the fact that 'music' is almost indefinable today, we shall be concentrating in this chapter on what is normally understood to be what a child might expect when he or she begins on a course of instrumental music lessons.

Defining 'dyslexia' is almost as hard – and liable to omission – as defining 'music', and it is likely to remain so until somebody discovers its root cause. Meanwhile, there must be as many variations of what we call dyslexia (or specific learning difficulties) as there are species of roses, but the general pattern of characteristics underlying dyslexia is as recognisable as roses are. It is customary to regard dyslexia as a bundle of problems that have to be circumvented, and it is often hard for a dyslexic, living in a world that is essentially non-dyslexic, to see it as anything else. Sometimes, however, it is worth asking how much the criteria laid down by non-dyslexics are worth. I believe that there is room in the world of music, perhaps particularly in the teaching of music, for a good deal of compromise.

I think that the majority of people who wonder whether music can help dyslexics are really wondering whether music can help the dyslexic *to behave more in a non-dyslexic way*. This attitude presupposes that non-dyslexics are somehow more valuable than dyslexics and completely ignores the wonderfully imaginative, creative and lively qualities that dyslexics often bring, particularly to the arts. There is a recurring theme in all the anecdotes quoted below: the children *wanted* to learn a musical instrument. They must have felt drawn to music. Researchers with adults have suggested that the appreciation of music is predominantly an attribute of the right hemisphere of the brain, being the hemisphere that processes pitch, melodic contour, tonal memory and timbre (Gordon, 1978; Borchgrevink, 1982; Overy, 2000; Schneider *et al.*, 2005). Overy *et al.* (2004) have also investigated whether or not children (of an average age of 6 years 4 months) show the same hemispheric specialisation. They suggest that this develops with age. The left hemisphere is mainly, though not exclusively, concerned with rhythm and the naming or identification of tunes. This is the logical side of the brain, the side that is needed for reading skills and spelling. It would be natural for the dyslexic child to be inclined to right-brain activities, which would probably include music, art, acting and sport. These children are likely to be drawn towards a skill that is more compatible with their inclinations than logical left-brain skills, such as reading and writing. Many dyslexics wish that they were not dyslexic because of the difficulties they have with left-brain skills, but there are also many who have learnt to be happy with the way they are. As one of these said to me: 'I'm used to the way I am now and I wouldn't have me any different.'

Unfortunately, there are dyslexics who have had a miserable time cooped up with intimidating and unhelpful instrumental music teachers who have had a thoroughly negative and sometimes actually detrimental effect on their pupil's self-esteem. This, as we all know, is crucial for success in any field. Unless one is a fly on the wall, one cannot tell exactly why some children fail to gain anything very much from their music lessons while others gain a lot. Maybe it is because those who fail are the children one does not often get told about! But it can also be a matter of personal chemistry between the teacher and the pupil. I believe that a child can sense almost immediately whether the teacher is truly sensitive and the right person for them. A pupil will respond positively, perhaps not at first, if they are dyslexic, because their negative experiences may have taught them to be cautious and to try to hide what their real feelings and difficulties are, but eventually, when it is obvious to them that the teacher is a friend who can be trusted.

It does happen that, sometimes, parents do not realise that a dyslexic is likely to have just as many problems, and possibly more, with learning to read and play music as they have with literacy in the classroom. The child has to be quite sure that they want to learn if they are going to succeed, and it is no good if the parents are just searching around for something else that their child can do that may not turn out to be the failure which everything else has been. I have heard of several parents who have thought that the main reason for subjecting their dyslexic child to one-to-one lessons with a music teacher was to teach them to concentrate. It is important that the musical experience has to be so compelling that the child wants to pursue it in spite of any difficulty they may have in achieving their aims.

However, there are many dyslexics for whom their music lessons have been the one beacon of hope in an otherwise dark and depressing learning experience. I once had a letter from the mother of a dyslexic flautist, who said that her daughter's flute playing was her *only* source of self-esteem. Since then, I have heard the same thing over and over again. I am sure that this is a scenario that many a parent of a dyslexic child would recognise.

For several years now, studies have been carried out on how music may be harnessed to help all children in many different ways. On the whole, however, there has been a relatively small amount of empirical research done in the field of music and dyslexia, particularly as to how the learning of music can assist the dyslexic in their general education. Kate Overy at Edinburgh University is one of the few who are now working in this field (Chapter 4). What we have learnt of the value of music for dyslexics has been chiefly anecdotal. Evidence of this comes pouring in, often uninvited but always welcome. The following stories are all illustrative of how music has changed the lives of the dyslexic pupils who were lucky enough to have the support and encouragement of teachers and parents. Sometimes a parent will decide that their dyslexic offspring has too much on their plate already to take on music lessons as well. These parents do not want to risk more failure. I suggest that if there were any evidence that the child is musical it would be a risk worth taking, as can be seen from the following stories.

Personal histories: increased self-esteem and confidence

Tim

Tim's story illustrates how any child can be set on fire by a particular sort of sound to the extent that, *whatever their difficulties*, they will pursue it until they have mastered the skill to create that sound for themselves. Having discovered that something which initially seemed so difficult was actually accessible if he tried hard enough, Tim seems to have been reassured that other skills would come his way if he persevered.

Tim began learning the cello aged 7. At that time his parents were watching their bright, happy, communicative little boy failing to cope at school, struggling with literacy, getting a lot of negative vibes because teachers said he was being lazy and also clearly far less able than his older brother and sister. His major dyslexic difficulties were, and still are, with poor visual memory and information-processing speed. At that time his state primary school employed peripatetic music teachers. He heard other children playing the cello and decided that he too wanted to learn because he loved its deep resonant sound. His class teacher, the school music specialist, said that he would never cope with an instrument, but the cello teacher said she would teach him if that was what he wanted, but not if the impetus came from the parents.

Tim started really slowly. He found rhythm difficult and his sequential memory made it hard for him to learn a tune. Quite how he stuck it out, when other more successful learners gave up, his mother said she would never know, except that he is a determined character and he really loved the rich sound. His teacher started him reading music from quite early on, in spite of the fact that he had difficulty tracking a line of print in a book. His mother thought that the combination of reading the note and making a physical action to play it before moving on to the next note really helped with tracking. His teacher was extremely supportive, even though she previously knew very little about dyslexia, and his music lessons came to be a real highlight in what was often a difficult and unrewarding week. With a less sensitive teacher, things could have been very different. Although he was not outstandingly good at the cello, he was starting to develop a skill in which he could take pride and which was not shared by most of his class.

Tim started to read stories more fluently between the ages of 8 and 9. His mother does not know how much of this was due to his music or how much it was due to a lot of literacy support at home, or whether it would have happened anyway, but she thinks it would not have. Although he is now hoping to read history at university, he has kept up his music, as it gives him a great deal of satisfaction and pleasure. He is going to take Grade 7 before he leaves school. His mother thinks that his cello lessons were useful both for the discipline of sequential activity (music reading and scale learning) and for building his self-esteem. She says: 'Music was the first thing that ever went right at school.'

Andrew

Andrew's story illustrates the individuality of the dyslexic learner. It also sheds another light on the importance of finding the right teacher who is prepared to take risks and allow a child to learn the way they can and not the way that is usually taught.

Andrew began to learn the cello when he was 5 years old, before anyone realised that he was dyslexic. His teacher was a very enthusiastic lady and liked his mother to be present during his lessons so that he had extra support when he was practising at home. Both his teacher and his mother encouraged and praised him together. He started learning the piano a year later and seemed to absorb reading music without any difficulty, but his teacher did not insist on his knowing the names of the notes at that stage.

Everything changed when the family moved abroad because of his father's job. The teaching was now very formal and his new piano teacher insisted on his knowing what the notes were called before he was allowed to play them. He found this very difficult because when required to focus on lines and spaces he would be unable to decide exactly where the note was. He soon gave up the piano, though he did manage to keep the cello going. These were not happy days, and his parents were worried about the way his love of music lessons was falling off.

Eventually, the family moved back to England and things began to look up again. School was hard: Andrew was no good at games, he could not catch a ball and big numbers confused him. (When his mother asked him what he meant by 'big numbers', he said: 'Anything over three!') He was not unintelligent; his mother explained the binary system to him and he picked it up immediately and now uses it in his work all the time. But music was something he could *excel* at. He joined a local youth orchestra and eventually achieved Grade 8 on the cello. Playing the cello had been a lifeline for him.

Jenny

Jenny's story is about a girl who was very sensitive to her own shortcomings but, like Tim, was so captivated by the sound of the cello that she was prepared to lay herself open to the possibility of more failure in the hope that one day she would succeed in being able to play it well enough to be able to join in music-making with others. In admitting her fears and her ambitions, and with the help of caring and supportive teachers who believed in her, she eventually tasted success, not only in music but in other fields too.

Jenny was very apprehensive about starting at a new school and confessed to her cello teacher that she was afraid that she would not be able to read music. She said she found reading words difficult, but someone in her family had played the cello and she liked the sound of it enough to want to try it herself. She had had very little help with her dyslexic problems at her previous school and had been considered quite backward, but actually she was an intelligent child who did not learn the way she was expected to learn. She learnt differently, as all dyslexics do.

Jenny's first lesson began with a simple multisensory demonstration of minims and crotchets followed by an explanation of the four open strings and where the notes that corresponded to them could be found on the stave. She sailed through the lesson reading everything that was put in front of her and left the room having, for the first time in her life, made sense of written information quickly and easily.

Fortunately for Jenny, the school had a strong support system for dyslexics, and over the years her cello teacher and her support teacher worked closely together, noting everything that was going on. The support teacher was positive that Jenny benefited enormously both from the one-to-one tuition on the cello and also from playing in groups for concerts because she had acquired a sense of her own worth. She also thought that Jenny gained valuable auditory support through learning to play a musical instrument and had increased her powers of auditory perception.

Personal histories: being part of a team

Jonathan

Jonathan, another dyslexic from a musical family, learnt the trumpet and the drums. He always had trouble reading music, but when he was at secondary school he was taken to see an optometrist who prescribed eye exercises to help him to focus better. Eventually, he was able to join a band that had a very supportive leader and he enjoyed being part of a team that actually achieved things. Music mattered more to him than anything else; it was something he *could* do. He actually achieved Grade 8 on the trumpet. His mother said that 'music kept him together' and also, very tellingly, that 'music speaks to the emotions when all else has failed'.

Ian

Ian was labelled a 'slow learner' at school in the days before dyslexia was recognised as a condition that needed appropriate remedial treatment. He realises now that he has always been dyslexic, partly because he also has a dyslexic son. He struggled academically, but music was a refuge and a confidence builder for him. His piano teacher was 'great'. She seemed to have an understanding that he would 'get it eventually', and the school band was also run well; so he took up the clarinet and loved playing with others even though the music was often way above his playing ability. He felt that he could contribute as part of a team and later he realised that this team spirit was very significant because he became conscious that people need to be able to work as part of a team throughout life. He is convinced from his own experience that music can help dyslexics, and his conviction is such that he has now become a music teacher himself, specialising in children with learning difficulties.

Personal histories: improving concentration

Tracey

Ian has analysed the effect which music has had on his own life. Tracey, who is still in her early teens, has also thought about how music has influenced her life so far. She used to be a bit of a rebel at school, but she thinks that learning to play the piano has calmed her because her piano teacher sets her short-term goals that she can achieve, and she enjoys the success. She thinks that her concentration has improved because she has such a desire to learn new pieces and, at her request, her teachers in the classroom are giving her more achievable short-term goals to keep her focused in other subjects. This seems to be working. Her piano teacher has also encouraged her to read about her pieces and their composers and Tracey says that this has helped her English.

James

I have written about James before (Oglethorpe, 2001). Following the extremely moving and fruitful experience that I had when I heard his story, both he and his mother kept in touch with me. He had become a cathedral chorister two or three years later than the normal age, which can be as early as 7 years old, but it was an enormous struggle for him at first. He could not tell the time or sequence the days of the week and so did not know which day of the week it was or what happened on that day, and he was unable to follow the timetable. But music was what he lived for, and the discipline of the chorister life was extremely beneficial for him. When his voice broke, the benefits of his choristership continued through his teens. He thinks that he had become so accustomed to reading music and the words of hymns, psalms and anthems that he transferred the skill to reading books. The desire to read has stayed with him and he is now at university. This is not to say that his dyslexia is, for want of a better word, cured, far from it, but, as most usually happens with dyslexics, and often at great cost, he has learnt to cope.

Mark

There is a parallel between James and Mark, also a cathedral chorister. Mark was awarded a choral scholarship to a very prestigious cathedral. He had already been diagnosed as dyslexic but had also had an intelligence test from an educational psychologist, who found that he had an exceptionally high IQ and advised that he should be educated as far as possible with other very intelligent children. It was suggested to the headmaster of the choir school that Mark was so intelligent that he would eventually find his own way to get round his problems, and the fact that he was dyslexic should not be allowed to stand in his way. Both the choirmaster and the headmaster were prepared to take the risk.

Mark's chief problem was that his auditory memory for speech was very short. He needed to watch the teacher speak. He also found that he was unable to pitch sounds by interval, but, having once heard the sound, however difficult, he could pick it out of the air with no trouble; so he was invaluable in the choir whenever really modern music was performed. Concentration was a problem, very probably because of his short verbal memory; so he found it hard to maintain an argument, and he did not do well academically in his early years. However, he did well enough eventually to get a degree at Cambridge University, and he is now head of his department at a large comprehensive school. It is difficult to quantify the main benefit that his musical education had on his academic prowess, but it seems that it was chiefly a huge improvement in his power of concentration.

Personal histories: auditory perception

Simon

I have already mentioned that Jenny's auditory perception improved when she started cello lessons. Simon had been receiving learning support for some time when he began learning the cello aged 7. He had two older siblings, both of them dyslexic, and a very supportive family. In his early childhood he had suffered a series of ear infections just at the point when he should have been developing the ability to synthesise sounds, and his learning process had undoubtedly been affected. He was particularly adept at mathematics, but his dyslexia was serious enough to handicap him in all other fields of learning.

His teacher used her own multisensory method to teach Simon about note lengths, which he picked up immediately, and she found that fingering was much less of a problem than for most of his peers because of his apparent affinity with numbers. As he had no alphabetical system in his head, however, letter names of notes were totally meaningless. His teacher felt that at least he ought to be familiar with the letter names of the open strings; so she decided to relate them to people that were important to him, one of them being his father and one the cat! Letter names began to take on a character of their own. He began to read music easily, and when his teacher asked him why he found it so much easier than reading words he said: 'I think of it like numbers.'

Simon also became an unusually perceptive and reliable member of a cello group. This made it possible for him to participate in something that he enjoyed, and on an equal footing with his peers.

It was only a short time, about two terms, before the dyslexia support teacher noticed a huge change in Simon's auditory perception that affected his reading and spelling.

Conclusion

There may be no empirical evidence of music lessons helping dyslexics. Experience does show, however, that the musical dyslexic child who has been allowed and encouraged to develop their talent is likely to find that what they have learnt in the music room is reflected in the classroom. Music can assist with the learning of the basics of the literary process by increasing awareness of sequential activity, by improving auditory perception (which helps with reading and spelling), by emphasising the importance of accurate tracking, and by providing encouragement to read. In addition there is some anecdotal evidence that the improvement which is engendered from the finger dexterity that is required for many instruments can improve the handwriting of some dyslexics. Also, because of the precise nature of written music and the extraordinary complexity of the mix of time, rhythm, pitch, dynamics and style, as one parent said, 'music hooks them in to concentrate'.

There are any number of stories about dyslexic children who have developed a sense of their own worth, as Jenny did. By learning to play a musical instrument, a child can contribute to the creation of a musical experience with his or her peers. This, of course, is extremely valuable in itself, not least because dyslexia is such an isolating condition. The dyslexic person seems so often to be running an obstacle race while everyone else is running a flat race. There seems to be no doubt that, if the dyslexic child is musical and has the right teacher, one of the main advantages of instrumental music lessons is the boost to children's self-esteem when they are able to create for themselves the joy of music. This has been another recurring theme in all the stories I have come across. Success can begin in the first lesson and can be built upon with none of the stresses of competition that are inevitably experienced in the classroom. Eventually, when playing alongside other children or taking part in an instrumental ensemble, another dimension begins that gives enormous satisfaction: the awareness of being part of a team with something unique to contribute. The value of this is inestimable. Enabling a child to enjoy the satisfaction of partaking in a shared musical experience, where everyone has their own particular obstacles to overcome before the job can be completed and where everyone has to be sensitive to what is being created all the time, gives them a taste of that real comradeship which is so often lacking in the rest of their uphill struggle.

References

Borchgrevink, H.M. (1982) Prosody and musical rhythm are controlled by the speech hemisphere. In M. Clynes (ed), *Music, Mind and Brain: The Neuropsychology of Music*, Plenum Press, New York.

Gordon, H.W. (1978) Hemispheric asymmetry for dichotically-presented chords in musicians and non-musicians, males and females. *Acta Psychologica* **42**(5): 383–395.

Oglethorpe, S. (2001) The dyslexic chorister. In: *Music and Dyslexia: Opening New Doors*, T.R. Miles and J. Westcombe (eds), Whurr, London.

Overy, K. (2000) Dyslexia, temporal processing and music: the potential of music as an early learning aid for dyslexic children. *Psychology of Music* **28**(2): 218–229.

Overy, K. Norton, A.C., Cronin, K.T. *et al.* (2004) Imaging melody and rhythm processing in young children. *Neuro Report* **15**(11): 1723–1726.

Schneider, P., Sluming, V., Roberts, N., Bleeck, S. and Rupp, A. (2005) Structural, functional, and perceptual differences in Heschl's Gyrus and musical instrument preference. *Annals of the New York Academy of Sciences* **1060**(1): 387–394.

eight

Parallels between the teaching of musical and mathematical notation

Tim Miles

The aim of this chapter is to show some of the similarities between what is needed in the teaching of musical notation and the teaching of mathematical notation. It is, of course, possible to play and listen to music without a knowledge of its notation, whereas the learning of mathematics cannot even start without a knowledge of the function of the symbols 1, 2, 3 etc. It is widely agreed, however, that those without a knowledge of musical notation are foregoing many of the pleasures of music-making, including the possibility of playing or singing in a huge variety of groups as well as individual work. They may also miss out on the possibility of making a detailed study of a musical score and hence of coming to a better understanding of the composer's intentions.

Musicians who are dyslexic are likely to need more time than those who are not dyslexic to master the intricacies of musical notation – just as they need more time to master the notation which we call letters of the alphabet. I am quite sure, however, that for the very great majority of dyslexics who are keen on music the effort involved in mastering musical notation is well worth while.

What, then, are the parallels between teaching musical notation and teaching mathematical notation?

There is in the first place an interesting difference between the two notations. In the notation of basic mathematics the instructions as to what is to be done are specified to the last detail; in contrast, in musical notation there remains much that is left to the interpretation of the performer. For example, the composer may write the instruction *rallentando*, which means 'slow down'. Exactly how much to slow down, however, in order to give the best effect, is something which has to be decided by the performer. It is a matter of familiar experience that we may regard one person's interpretation of a piece of music as superior to that of another person's. In contrast, if the notation in basic mathematics tells us to carry out a particular calculation the answer is either right or wrong. One proof of a theorem may, indeed, be more elegant than another, and to that extent there is room for preference. There can be no preference, however, as to whether we say $2 + 2 = 4$ or $2 + 2 = 5$; the latter is wrong – full stop.

In the case of speech, one can usefully think of letters of the alphabet as things which in combination tell us what mouth movements to use. Similarly, one can think of numerals as instructions as to what to say in order to tell people how many objects are present or the length of a distant object in space or time. Similarly, one can think of musical notation as a set of instructions telling us what notes to play on a musical instrument or what notes to sing. In all these cases there is an association between marks on paper and muscular movements.

There is a rather curious linguistic convention by which the expression 'the music' sometimes refers not to music as such but to the musical score. Thus, if someone asks, 'Have you brought the music?' this is understood to mean the written version of the music, for instance the piano or orchestral parts or the parts of a piece of chamber music. In view of this linguistic convention, it is very important that the difference between music and musical notation should be recognised from the very start by both dyslexic pupils and their teachers. This is primarily because a dyslexic pupil may find the decoding of musical notation very hard but yet be an extremely sensitive musician.

Those who teach mathematics to dyslexics and those who teach them music have to deal with what are basically the same problems. It is less easy for a dyslexic than for a non-dyslexic to attach the right name to a particular symbol. As was pointed out in Chapter 1, dyslexia essentially involves a problem with naming, or verbal labelling. This is true whether the thing to be named is a letter of the alphabet, an Arabic numeral, a square-root sign or a chemical formula. It is also true in the case of a clef sign, the symbols signifying duration, such as crotchets and minims, a time signature, an instruction saying 'da capo' and, in general, the whole range of signs which go to make up musical notation. In all cases learning the name of the symbol is possible for dyslexics, but it may take them more time and effort than it takes their non-dyslexic peers: the names may take longer to sink in and become associated with their meaning, and may also be more easily forgotten. Once, however, the names have been learnt, dyslexics are no worse than non-dyslexics at applying what they know.

With regard to the notation of mathematics, all children in our educational system are required to learn the Arabic numerals 1, 2, 3 etc. and the signs for multiplication ($\times$), division ($\div$), addition ($+$) and subtraction ($-$). As they advance, they have to learn the use of further symbols, such as the equals sign ($=$), the sign for square root ($\sqrt{}$) and, in due course, other symbols such as Π, cosine and many more.

Those symbols that are in frequent use, when they have once been acquired, stay in the memory. This is true of dyslexics and non-dyslexics alike. It is particularly so if the number of symbols in a given list is small, for example the days of the week. A dyslexic child may be relatively late in learning to recite them but is unlikely to have any long-lasting difficulty. In contrast, the months of the year require the learning and ordering of 12 names, and these come round relatively infrequently compared with the days of the week. This means that for some dyslexic children the knowledge is not secure until their teens or even later. The spelling of long words and the recitation of arithmetical tables both impose a heavy load on the memory system, which means that, without special effort or special compensatory strategies, a dyslexic child may go through life without, for instance, being able to recite some of the more awkward times tables, such as the six, seven, eight and 12 times. (The 10 and 11 times have obvious regularities, and the nine times is possible if one remembers that its digits always add up to a multiple of nine ($0 + 9$, $1 + 8$, $2 + 7$, $3 + 6$ etc.).

It is sometimes possible, however, because dyslexic pupils and their teachers are aware of such limitations, that in particular areas they may invest extra time and effort in acquiring a particular skill and end up being *more* proficient than some non-dyslexics. Thus, although most dyslexic musicians are relatively weak at sight-reading, I know of a dyslexic double bass player, Michael Lea (see Chapter 11), who finds that his sight-reading is better than average. To say simply that a dyslexic *cannot* do this or that has always seemed to me unnecessarily defeatist.

How, then, can the learning of arithmetical or musical terms best be taught? It is widely agreed that, whatever the symbols in question – letters of the alphabet, numerals and the symbols used in musical notation – simply relying on the pupil's memory is ineffective. The teaching needs first and foremost to be multisensory.

'Multisensory' means 'involving many senses'; in other words, in multisensory teaching one does not teach through vision alone or through hearing alone. The pupil is encouraged to look carefully at the symbol, to listen carefully to its sound, to pay attention to the mouth movements needed for saying its name and to the hand movements needed for writing or typing it. If all these senses work in conjunction, memorisation becomes much easier.

Secondly, the teaching needs to take advantage of the dyslexic's strengths. Dyslexics tend to be good at reasoning and, once the names of the symbols have been acquired, at doing creative things with them and at recognising regularities and patterns.

Because any notation is likely to present dyslexics with difficulty, it is understandable if they find learning it unpleasant. An important starting point, therefore, is to make them aware that both mathematics and music are things to be enjoyed. That is why it is not good practice to allow them to associate either mathematics or music with the, to them, laborious task of learning notations. A teacher who says to the class (I hope none do!), 'We are going to do music this morning. Learn this: E-G-B-D-F' may give the impression to dyslexic children that music is not for them.

In the case of mathematics there are all kinds of ways of creating enjoyment. For the very young child it may be enjoyable just to play with blocks and build things with them. If the blocks are differently coloured, there is the opportunity to build all sorts of patterns – and it should be remembered that many dyslexics are artistically gifted, and so, in the example of the coloured blocks, one is encouraging them to use their strengths.

By the same token, music is something to be enjoyed. For some young children, it can be fun simply to beat on a drum or make a noise with castanets. At a later age many dyslexic children, like other children, may derive pleasure from listening to music and from playing tunes by ear (that is without any notation) on a piano, recorder or other instrument.

Notation, whether mathematical, musical or any other, needs to be introduced to dyslexic children only very gradually, with plenty of time being allowed for them to take it in; otherwise they will not remember it. It is unhelpful to come up with remarks such as, 'I showed you that yesterday – why didn't you listen?'

When the notation to be learnt is mathematical, the teacher may like to set out blocks in groups of, say, three, four or five, and ask the pupil to count them. As was indicated above, learning the names of the Arabic numerals from 1 to 10 and writing them down is a manageable task for the young dyslexic, provided they are not rushed. Similarly, there is little difficulty in associating the names of the numerals with the correct number of objects – blocks, animals, trees etc. However, a dyslexic may be at risk of missing out on one or more stages of the learning process, and it is important that teachers check that this has not happened. Constant revision is virtually essential.

The teacher can then ask the pupil to put, say, two blocks on the table, add a further three blocks and then count up how many blocks there are altogether. Then, when the pupil has really grasped what is happening, the teacher can say, 'Now, shall we write down for the benefit of someone else what we have been doing? Write this number' (point to a group of two blocks); 'now write this number' (point to a group of three blocks); 'and now write this number' (point to the five blocks in combination). When the pupil has understood what is happening, it is then possible to introduce the symbols '+' (add) and '−' (take away). All this needs to be done slowly and systematically, with the pupil aware of the actual blocks being added or taken away.

Symbols for 'multiply' and 'divide' can then be introduced, with explanations such as 'two lots of three' or 'Share these blocks between six children'. The important point is that all this is done *after* the real-life event has taken place and its significance understood. What is daunting for dyslexic children is confronting them with a mass of symbols and not giving them enough time even to learn their names, let alone appreciate their function. New symbols should always be introduced in an orderly and systematic way.

Readers may also like to know that there is now in existence multisensory software (Flynn, 1998), with which it is possible for the learner to control the movement of blocks in a three-dimensional environment. An account of what is happening is presented auditorily and the appropriate visual symbols appear, such as '+' and '=' and the requisite numerals.

One occasionally finds that even older dyslexic children have somehow missed out on the understanding of these basic mathematical principles, and in Miles (2004) ways in which structured materials such as Dienes blocks can be used to promote understanding are suggested. At this stage, too, it is possible to show the pupil that mathematics is something to be enjoyed. Our number system contains all kinds of regularities and patterns, for instance the fact that the successive multiples of three are alternately odd and even numbers. Many dyslexics are interested in such things and are likely to find the discovery of new patterns and regularities very enjoyable.

What, then, can be learnt from all this about the teaching of musical notation?

It seems clear in the first place that those who teach music to dyslexic pupils of all ages should make them aware of the difference between music and musical notation: if they experience difficulty with the notation, this does not mean that they are incompetent musicians. It is also important that musical notation should be taught slowly and systematically and that the dyslexic learner should be allowed plenty of time for the words and symbols (marks on the stave signifying pitch, clef signs, time signatures etc.) to sink in. A multisensory approach is described by Hubicki (2001), and it is hoped that actual materials will be appearing on the market in the not-too-distant future. In the meantime, teachers may like to join with the pupil in creating their own materials. These can be adapted according to the pupil's needs. It may be enjoyable, for instance, for a young pupil to draw five lines so as to construct a stave, write in the appropriate clef sign, write a succession of notes on the stave – perhaps, say, two crotchets in the first place, then, later, some minims, quavers etc. If one writes, for example, two crotchets on the stave, paying attention to one's hand movements in writing them, and then looks at the two marks on the stave and plays on an instrument a succession of two notes, listening to each other carefully, there is likely to be better memorisation than if the pupil stares at a visual mark in isolation, listens to a sound in isolation and writes nothing down.

Cardboard and glue may be useful so that the shapes of the symbols can be handled. Pupils should speak the names of the symbols aloud as they handle them and should listen carefully to the sound of their own voice as well as to the sounds of the notes which they have written.

The familiar mnemonics ('Every good boy deserves food', 'Always come early Grandma' etc.) can, of course, be used. In addition, however, it is possible to take advantage of dyslexics' skill in recognising regularities and patterns. In her original Colour Staff, Hubicki (2001) gave each of the notes from A to G a different colour, corresponding to the colours of the spectrum – red, orange, yellow, green, blue, purple (indigo) and violet. Her intention was not to provide a new colour code – this would have been an extra load on the dyslexic's memory – but rather to highlight regularities of pattern. This is done by placing strips of coloured material on the lines and spaces of the stave. Thus, low G in the bass clef, which falls on a line, is coloured orange and low A, just above it, is coloured green. The next time the colour orange appears it is to represent the G immediately below middle C. All notes G are coloured orange, all notes A green and so on. It will be noted that low G, which is on a line, requires a narrow strip, while the G above, which is on a space, requires a wide strip. There is the same regularity of pattern in the treble clef and in any ledger lines above the stave.

In the case of more advanced players who needed the alto or tenor clefs, the same principles can be applied. The order of the colours in the spectrum is allowed for, since orange is a fifth above red, yellow is a fifth above orange, green is a fifth above yellow and so on.

Once the function of a symbol has been learnt, there is reason to think that the dyslexic is as capable as the non-dyslexic of putting that knowledge to good use. It is therefore particularly important that a musically gifted dyslexic should not be put off taking up music because of early difficulties in the learning of musical notation.

References

Flynn, S.J.O. (1998) *The Multimedia Interactive Calculator*, Inclusive Technology Ltd., Saddleworth Business Centre, Delph, Oldham, OL3 5DF.

Hubicki, M. (2001) A multisensory approach to the teaching of musical notation. In: *Music and Dyslexia: Opening New Doors*, T.R. Miles and J. Westcombe (eds), Whurr, London.

Miles, T.R. (2004) The use of structured materials with older pupils. In: *Dyslexia and Mathematics*, T.R. Miles and E. Miles (eds), RoutledgeFalmer, London.

nine

The paperwork

Diana Ditchfield

The paperwork watershed is often thought of as the Grade 5 theory examination. This is principally because it is often a qualifying requirement for proceeding to a Grade 6 practical examination. It is quite a reasonable examination if theory has been taught alongside, and preferably in tandem with, learning to play a musical instrument, and if theory has been steadily studied and examined. Some students take it in their stride; for others it becomes an insurmountable hurdle. For some dyslexic students it is a very stressful hurdle. I often tell my students that it is very easy to lose marks in theory – and usually these marks are lost on things you actually know; this is regardless of whether a student is dyslexic or not.

It is indeed true that it is often necessary to organise several types of information into one answer. For example, a question may require a student to: (a) write a melodic minor scale (b) in the above rhythm (c) ascending (d) with key signature (e) beginning on the third (or mediant) degree of the scale (f) in the tenor clef. This is fraught with traps for the *non*-dyslexic student, and so how much more for the dyslexic student, who may have weak organisational skills, be very anxious about doing an examination, may have already failed it twice, may not be very good with a pencil and/or writing between lines and has forgotten to bring a pencil/pen, rubber and pencil sharpener? In addition, they have forgotten a statement of dyslexia with the entry form, have arrived late because they muddled the time and have forgotten to bring their candidate number.

I recall individually teaching an intelligent and very musical 15-year-old boy who was an accomplished flute and violin player. He had an excellent ear and could 'hear' his melodies. When doing practice papers prior to the Grade 5 examination, he wrote an innovative but acceptable melody – until the last note, which was written G in the key of F. We had a good and relaxed relationship that had developed over some time where mutual trust was enjoyed; this allowed for the unbridled giving and receiving of criticism that never provoked any kind of resentment, and when I berated him, he replied, 'But you knew I meant F!' – which was perfectly true. He was somewhat clumsy with his pencil and it was not unusual for his notes to slip up or down or even cover lines and spaces. However, his writing of G was incorrect and should be penalised. I hoped that the statement of his dyslexia, which accompanied his entry form for the examination, would cover any error of this nature because a musical marker would be able to detect the good points of the melody attempt. In the event, he passed with a little to spare. Mindful that dyslexics often react particularly badly to the stress of examinations, it is possible they will make uncharacteristic mistakes in addition to those one might expect.

This scenario is merely a small part and a single example of some paperwork problems that may face the dyslexic musician. In this case, carefully structured cumulative, multisensory and steady and sensitive teaching – maybe individually, rather than in a class – should overcome any problems with the Grade 5 theory examination, especially if the entry is actually accompanied by a statement of dyslexia and maybe mentioning any special requirements. It is, of course, very important to teach in a dyslexic-friendly manner: examining/assessing must be adjusted according to the specific difficulties of the particular dyslexic. Obviously, speaking metaphorically, there is no point in building a wall unless each layer of bricks is firmly and correctly established from the foundation upwards. Personally, I have found it is sometimes helpful to use (not slavishly follow) Margaret Hubicki's Colour Staff (Ditchfield, 2001), particularly for ledger lines, and especially with students who learn an instrument where the music is written on a single clef. Sheila Oglethorpe (1996) has many suggestions about approaching teaching problems in her book *Instrumental Music for Dyslexics*. There are also sometimes alternative modes of assessment apart from sitting a conventional examination in theory – or, indeed, any other examination. Any assessment should inquire into the knowledge it is testing and not be a vehicle to discover or prove dyslexia.

However, a dyslexic musician often has many other paperwork difficulties apart from sitting the Grade 5 theory examination, and this chapter will comment on some of these and suggest ways of addressing them. The sad fact is that these paperwork requirements, such as essays or other written assignments, still preclude some music students and other individuals even getting onto the bottom rung of the ladder that leads to where they want to be. Possibly one of the most difficult tasks for the non-dyslexic helper of dyslexics is to understand how it is for them – and the dyslexic is always so encouraged when people do. It often amazes me to find the dyslexic so tolerant of, and even charitable to, those of us who cannot understand their differences. It must be appalling to feel a wall of concrete blocks in your way no matter how you try to find a way through. Whichever way you try to proceed, a difficulty gets in your way. You want to do it just as the non-dyslexic, not just to show others that you are not idiotic but also to go some way to getting where you want to be and doing what you know, deep down, that you are able to do – and all of that before achieving well beyond your own vision and realising your full potential. The frustration is unimaginable!

A dyslexic player of the French horn who attended a specialist music school at secondary level and then proceeded to a conservatoire never succeeded in gaining any qualifications of any description in terms of school certificates or music diplomas. When he taught in a music school, his student attendance register was certainly not suitable as a legal document and he needed a great deal of peer support to make it even legible. He felt very inadequate as a result and had to battle with problems associated with low self-esteem for many years. All this was in spite of the fact that he was enormously valued as an orchestral player and teacher. When he played a Mozart horn concerto in a large concert hall, the audience was completely transported.

Dyslexics want to achieve on the same playing field where their non-dyslexics peers get where they want, even though they know they may not fully demonstrate their real ability. Most dyslexics I know work at least twice as hard as many of their peers. They often go down blind alleys and take a very circuitous route to get on the road they seek. For many who try to express themselves, they have an idea of what they want to say/write but it does not come out in a format that makes sense; certainly it is often not in a format which is acceptable to the standards set down for success in the areas in which they are making the attempt.

Those who try to help dyslexics get where they want often have to fish around with the individual dyslexic to try and find out what it is they want to say and help them say it in the way they want – and this is often on a sentence-by-sentence basis, and all before any organisational structure is apparent. It often takes a great deal of time but it is a great privilege for the helper/supporter if/when the dyslexic is content with the ultimate end product. It means it is *their*, the dyslexic's, work which has resulted in *their own* success. At the time of writing, this contributor is in awe of a young dyslexic student who has just achieved a perfect first-class degree – in a discipline which is almost unintelligible to the helper/supporter. It *is* possible for dyslexics to handle the paperwork, but it is not easy.

Thus, self-esteem and self-confidence need to be fostered honestly. This often means dyslexia is not a secret any more, and that is often a difficult first hurdle for the dyslexic. Even those of us who have worked with dyslexia for many years still do not fully understand the individual problems associated with individual patterns of dyslexia; and how much more is this the case for those who are focused mostly on teaching their own subject, even if they are genuinely also trying to be student-centred. Some are more willing than others to make the effort and accommodate the 'deviancy' of dyslexia. In addition, there is a certain amount of trial and error by all involved in the teaching/learning experience. One fact which is often present and not fully appreciated is that dyslexics often take a lot longer to learn and rehearse information sufficiently for it to be securely stored in the long-term memory and be manipulated or reproducible. Peer and/or paired learning can be helpful for some; while others find it very stressful to work with others, even in group projects.

This non-dyslexic writer found co-ordinating the use of three organs, a treble and two bass clefs with two hands and two feet extremely confusing, especially when the pitch range of each and the vertical position of where the music was to be played compared with the written page was out of sync to her. Out of the blue, a colleague who overheard a verbal recital of the impossibility of playing the organ said, 'Think of the feet as playing in the tenor clef', and suddenly the problems receded considerably. It was an accidental success. I was reminded of trying to teach theory to a 7-year-old accomplished Suzuki violin player who seemed unable to understand that there were two minims in a semibreve and two crotchets in a minim and so on. The rest of the class escaped tummy ache in spite of eating many halves and quarters of apples for about six weeks. Suddenly, out of the blue, the young violin player announced, 'I understand, there are two half notes in a whole note.' I thought I had explained that! Realisation came when she was ready. The element of shooting in the dark should not be shunned by anybody.

Additionally, because dyslexics often process certain types of information more slowly than non-dyslexics, time should be allowed for it to be taken on board. If a lesson or lecture is proceeding quickly, a dyslexic may miss a second bit of information before the first bit of information has got sorted. In first and/or secondary school, the student may switch off and give up because any additional information that follows and requires the building block of the piece of information they have missed is nonsense to them; it adds to confusion and possibly distress. One effect is that these students may need extra time for assignments because they have to fill in the gaps afterwards, in one way or another. However, a delay in submitting assignments needs to be balanced against falling behind timetabled requirements where there is a limited degree of flexibility. Given the negative effect of stress on dyslexics (Miles and Varma, 1995; Peer, 2003), extra time should be available for examinations even if it is not taken up.

One of the first requirements is to help the helpers. The would-be helper needs the correct objectives concerning, and clear information about, the area being studied by the dyslexic student. This means information such as access to textbooks, lecture material, assessment requirements, lesson/seminar interaction – and this may imply video and/or audiotaped lessons or a peer note-taker. None of these needs is impossible, but they do need co-operation. Where a student programme is very full, it becomes imperative to carefully balance time and lifestyle and to make choices. Aural/oral presentation may be a useful and fair alternative tool, particularly if a musician is permitted to use a practical instrument to support them.

A further requirement is material that is accessible to the dyslexic. Sometimes, audio/videotaped music and musical scores, books and journals are needed. Assistive and information technology may be required; it is often expensive but it can make all the difference to the dyslexic. Larger print may be sufficient but the use of other aids such as coloured or computer-generated filters or, for example, Irlen lenses may be useful for some dyslexics. Where there are essay requirements, the ability to use a computer can change the picture entirely for some dyslexics. Although not infallible, Spell-check and syntactic support are often useful – as are calculators and the relatively free use of the photocopier. These supports can assist accuracy where there is risk of inaccuracy and its effects. However, it is worth remembering that sometimes the implication is that the student has, in effect, to study two courses – one in the subject being studied and the second in the use of the technology by which to access the former. The use of a reader and/or scribe may assist some dyslexics, although, in this case, additional physical space needs to be taken into consideration and the fact that the student has to be willing to be seen as being not the same as their peers.

There is a wealth of software that can help dyslexics with their theory work, including inputting speech into a document, for reading text and pointing to the errors of the dyslexic writer and helping them organise all aspects of their work. Having said that, some of the software is quite complicated and requires time to learn it or help with using it. Dragon and Kurzweil have been the tools for success for some dyslexics who would not have achieved otherwise. Computer Touch programs suit others. The music-processing system Sibelius has released musical creative gifts which would remain locked up in its absence. Computer structures such as the PowerPoint system, Excel or Access and others have helped some dyslexics, whereas they would be a confusing handicap for others. There are now too many to mention and these technologies are increasing and improving by the day; many are also age- and stage-related. When considering the dyslexic musician, it is appropriate that the emphasis should be on multisensory approaches.

One of the wonderful side effects of being dyslexic is being able, because of creative tendencies, to solve one's own problems. This writer recalls working with a 17-year-old exam student who was trying to remember a list of difficult but essential technical words. No attempt to provide a skeleton structure seemed useful and it was therefore a great shock the following week when the student was able to reproduce them all without error. When asked how she had done it, I was amazed to hear that she had devised her own ingenious mnemonic. Mnemonics are useful learning tools, although too many can simply add more confusion. It is also worth remembering that all individuals, whether dyslexic or not, favour some learning styles and strategies over others. While none should be excluded, where time and energy are limited it makes sense to use the favoured style. Success encourages success. However, in that there is a tendency for the dyslexic to have a focused way of taking information on board and reproducing it, it may be that a good teacher can suggest alternative approaches at times.

Is there a place for failure? This is a double-edged sword. When being interviewed for his contribution to Miles and Westcombe (2001), Nigel Clarke told of an experience when, early in his musical career, he knew he would fail an examination. He decided therefore that he might as well fail when using one of his own musical compositions. He *did* fail the examination. However, the examiner was diverted by the composition, and it was one of the milestones that helped Nigel embark on his successful career as a composer. Sometimes, failure can lead to an alternative route or goal where the eventual success may be exactly the same or much greater. It is a sensitive issue. People often unwittingly overwhelm dyslexics – even when that is the last thing they would want to do – and damage (sometimes irreparable) can be done. On the other hand, failure may be a pivotal experience in facing up to problems and obtaining the necessary help to prevent it in future.

A chapter of this length cannot be comprehensive. It is designed to raise paperwork problems that can affect dyslexic musicians and suggest they are not insurmountable if all concerned deal with them with realistically.

References

Ditchfield, D. (2001) Dyslexia and music. In: *Dyslexia: Successful Inclusion in the Secondary School*, L. Peer and G. Reid (eds), David Fulton/BDA, London.

Miles, T.R. and Varma, V. (eds) (1995) *Dyslexia and Stress*, Whurr, London.

Miles, T.R. and Westcombe, J. (eds) (2001) *Music and Dyslexia: Opening New Doors*, Whurr, London.

Oglethorpe, S. (1996) *Instrumental Music for Dyslexics: A Teaching Handbook*, Whurr, London.

Peer, L. (2003) Dyslexia: not a condition to die for. In: *The Dyslexia Handbook*, M. Johnson and P. Lindsay (eds), BDA, London.

ten

Sight-reading

Sheila Oglethorpe

Before we look at some ideas for helping dyslexic pupils with the peculiar challenges of sight-reading, it is worth noting that not *every* dyslexic pupil has more difficulty than a non-dyslexic pupil when learning to read at sight. There are some whose dyslexic traits affect them in areas of the brain that are not needed for sight-reading skills. For example, a dyslexic pupil may have an extremely short auditory memory for speech. This does not necessarily impinge on their ability to see a line of notes and reproduce the sounds on their instrument correctly. These lucky people are rare, although there is no doubt that they do exist.

Sight-reading words, sight-reading music

The process of learning to read music at sight has many more complications than learning to read words at sight, though the first two stages of reading either might be compared in a small way.

It is now widely agreed that the process of learning to read *words* at sight is roughly divided into three stages:

1. whole-pattern recognition
2. letter–sound conversion
3. the application of spelling rules and conventions.

It has been suggested (Frith, 1985) that dyslexics are delayed in reaching the second stage (letter–sound conversion).

It can be argued that for music there is no stage one, no pattern recognition. The beginner reader of text has little words like 'and', 'the', 'is' and so on that will have to be learnt as a whole word without analysing why they sound the way they do. There is no direct parallel for the beginner sight-reader of music; they have to go straight to stage two, letter (or symbol) to sound conversion, which is the very stage that dyslexic readers of text find so difficult to reach. In addition to analysing the pitch of the notes, there are the complications of the pulse beat and the rhythm, not to mention all the performance directions and so on.

Patient, systematic teaching in the classroom is likely to get a dyslexic pupil to a reasonable standard of proficiency in reading. If sight-reading music were as important to everyday life as is reading text, then perhaps the same amount of time and energy and patient systematic teaching applied to music would produce as much fluency as it does for sight-reading words. Sight-reading music is possible, but it needs a huge amount of dedication. However, not being able to sight-read adequately is not a bar to learning to play a piece of music, and there is no correspondence between musical talent and fluency in sight-reading.

Preparation

We know that reading well at sight is only achieved after a great deal of practice, but there are some who have seemingly impenetrable difficulties. Good preparation in all the normally accepted ways (choosing a sensible pulse beat, noting the time and key signature, looking out for accidentals, articulation and so on) should be undertaken *if it is feasible* but not necessarily when the pupil has an extremely poor short-term memory, which many dyslexics have. Too much time spent on this is not worth the trouble and can actually be counter-productive because it is so demoralising for a dyslexic when in performance they forget everything they have so painstakingly prepared. Dyslexics who are terrified of making mistakes and paralysed by the sight of a piece of music which they cannot recognise as a tune really need to learn to get on with it and not worry too much. More practice at this is a better expenditure of their energy than all that careful preparation.

Orientation at the keyboard

Many things are involved when sight-reading (courage being one of them!) but the more I see and hear of dyslexic pianists the more I believe that those with the worst problems are the ones who have been taught to work out all the letter names of the notes before playing them. For the player of a wind instrument with only one line of notes to follow, it is probably essential to know the letter names. These should be taught multisensorily, of which more later, but for a pianist, provided that they know how to *find* the notes on the keyboard in each hand, it is my belief that knowing what they are *called* is actually superfluous. The only way to cope is to listen and read by interval.

It is confusing and slow when sight-reading to work out what the letter name of every note is, for two reasons: (1) the treble and bass staves refer to a different set of letter names and (2) there are lots of Gs, on the keyboard, for example – which is the correct one? To overcome this, the dyslexic must have a readily accessible point of reference. In other words, they must know where they are.

The quickest way to find notes on the keyboard in the early stages is to home in on the middle lines in both clefs. The pupil should sit centrally at the keyboard with hands dangling at their sides. Next, the hands are lifted onto the keyboard in a direct forward line from the dangling position. They will automatically land either on, or extremely near, the bass and treble middle line notes. The left-hand D is the easier to identify because of the neat way it sits between the two black notes. The right-hand B is harder to remember, and pupils need to be encouraged to use their own imagination to help them establish firmly in their minds exactly where it is. (It can be useful later on to point out that if there is one flat in the key signature it is going to be the nearest black note to that B and all other Bs on the keyboard. Letter names will inevitably creep in, and so they should, but at this stage it is still unnecessary to know what they are. Knowing that the first flat is the highest of the three black notes group will do.)

Sight-reading material

Having established a link between the middle line in each clef, and where to place the hands on the keyboard, the very best material for sight-reading at the beginning, in order to create that sense of security from which more adventurous music can emanate, is invariably that which the teacher has tailor-made for the pupil he or she knows really well. Many excellent sight-reading books are on the market, but keep these for later on when the pupil has begun to feel that it may be difficult but not impossible.

Sight-reading with hands together

The teacher should write plenty of tunes using only the lines on the staves, hands together but not going outside a five-note compass at first. The pupil scans through the piece in order to identify the highest and the lowest notes in both hands so that they can decide which fingers to start with.

The initial aim should be to enforce the recognition of thirds and fifths. The tunes should be written on jumbo-sized manuscript paper and kept extremely short – not more than four bars long, thereby making it possible for the sight-reader to see the end and, with luck, not make too many errors. Every time the pupil manages to complete a four-bar exercise correctly will be a step towards greater confidence. When, with reading hands together, recognition of thirds and fifths on lines has been established, it is a fairly simple matter to transfer to the same idea using the spaces, though one does come across the dyslexic pupil who prefers either one or the other. Only when the pupil is happy using both lines and spaces should passing notes be incorporated. Very gradually, other intervals can be brought into play, but these should always be practised with hands together so that the habit of reading hands in both clefs at once becomes more and more automatic.

Key signatures

All foundations for good sight-reading have to be laid at the start of the process of learning to read music. Unfortunately, it is only too easy to overload a dyslexic pupil with information for which they seem to have no appropriate storage space in the memory. Careful consideration should be given to what to teach and what to leave out. Time signatures are, of course, very important, as are key signatures. It is frequently the key signature that gives the most trouble when sight-reading, but there is a very simple pattern on the keyboard which holds good for all the first five sharps or flats. For sharps, the order starts with the lowest of the three black notes group, followed by the lowest of the two black notes group, which is followed by the next lowest of each group in zigzag fashion until all the black notes are used up. For flats, the process starts with the highest note of the groups and works in reverse. Knowing this means that the pupil just has to count the number of flats or sharps in the key signature and rehearse them on the keyboard without worrying about their names. They can also easily work out what the keynote of the piece is by going to the nearest white note above the last sharp they have just played, or, for flats, by going back one black note from the end of the zigzag pattern that they have just worked out. F major is the exception, as there is only one black note. If the pupil puts their third finger on it and then slides it down onto the white note a semitone below and adds the first and fifth finger, they have made the key chord. Dyslexics should be reminded that it is the *lowest* note of the triad that gives the chord its name. The chord stands on its letter name.

Rhythm

Quite often, a dyslexic pupil will find that the rhythm of the piece is the most difficult aspect to grasp. Tapping or clapping it first can be helpful, for all instrumentalists, but asking a dyslexic to count aloud at the same time is often too much. By all means, set the beat going with a steady tap of the foot, but numbers are best left out of the exercise. Having noted what indications of speed the composer has written at the beginning of the piece, the sight-reader then has to decide which speed they are capable of achieving. Before setting out, it is essential to think through the whole of at least one bar, establishing the steady pulse beat. Whatever the instrument, it may be a good idea to have some sort of rehearsal first, not of the whole piece but at least of the bit that looks the most difficult. String players can pluck the tune through before adding the complications of bowing. Woodwind players can finger the notes without blowing. This practice is not, unfortunately, any good for brass players, but at least they should look out for danger areas and may need to clap rhythms.

Co-ordination on the piano

Sometimes a piano pupil who has difficulty understanding how what is going on in one hand fits with what is going on in the other may find it helpful, even amusing, to turn the music on its side. Provided that it is turned 90 degrees in a clockwise direction, it can then be read down the page in columns. What is seen on the right is then tapped by the right hand while the left hand taps the notes on the left. It is unlikely that the dyslexic will want to perform with the music in this position, but it can help them to get a feel for how the hands co-ordinate. Whichever way up it is, it is surprising how often the note tails seem to interfere with how the pupil perceives the synchronisation of the hands. You can sometimes alleviate this by suggesting that they mark with a highlighter pen where the hands play together in a tricky bit.

Learning note names multisensorily

Returning to note names, the woodwind player who equates the letter name of a note and its position on the stave with a particular fingering must be absolutely sure of both before reading at sight proficiently is a possibility. Many a pupil will have learnt to play a piece of music kinaesthetically, that is they will have taught their fingers what to do, without having really grasped what the notes are called. They will recognise what it *feels like* to produce the sounds that make up the tune, but may well flounder when required to play just the same sounds in a different order and rhythm. They may have learnt the progression of finger movements but not considered the names of the notes beyond the point where they were originally worked out, particularly in a descending passage where the alphabet is sequenced backwards. The brass player tends to be guided much more than other instrumentalists by their ear, and the pianist by their spatial ability, but it is very important for the woodwind player that all letter names of notes be over-learned until they are established beyond doubt.

A multisensory approach is the best way to instil confidence with letter names, and a stave drawn on the floor with masking tape is one of the best tools one can use. 'Jump to a B on a line! Jump to an E in a space! Jump to the octave E below!' There are many ways to use this aid, all of which can be fun. If the space is not available, one can make a board with felt, or hardboard, and place felt or Plasticine notes on it, but this is not as good as the floor stave because it is less multisensory: the whole body is not involved. I also use a metal tray on which I have the representation of a stave and little magnetic discs to represent notes. These can be easily and cleanly moved around, perhaps to spell words or to make tunes and so on. Whatever method of learning the note names is used, it is always important to equate them with the sounds and intervals they represent.

Making music

There is not time to do everything. A dyslexic person who is more worried about the notes should try to get used to leaving some of them out rather than allow the pulse beat to suffer. For pianists, duets can be extremely helpful in encouraging this. For other instrumentalists, some accompaniment is highly recommended. The exercise then begins to feel more like making music. Some pupils respond well when it is suggested that they just play the first note in each bar. It helps them to track through a line of music to the next strong beat without worrying. Strongly rhythmic music is best for this. Gradually, they can be encouraged to fill in the other beats, but only step by step, not attempting too much at a time and still leaving out anything that they do not feel ready for.

All the strategies to alleviate difficulties with the score that a teacher would normally use for a dyslexic pupil (enlarging, printing onto coloured paper etc.) should also be used when teaching sight-reading. Note that such aids can now be used in examinations too. The Associated Board of the Royal Schools of Music (2007), in its 'Guidelines for candidates with dyslexia or other learning difficulties', allows for such things as large notation tests, larger font for performance directions, tinted overlays or coloured paper and also extra time for preparation.

To suggest that the implementation of the ideas above is going to create good sight-readers among all dyslexic pupils would be to hold out false hopes and engender false expectations. One simply has to try everything and see what works best. Fear of the unknown can be so paralysing, and so one has to offer the dyslexic something that they can hold onto and which will give them that very necessary courage to go on. One never knows what is going to trigger the unlocking of a door, but everything that one can think of, or possibly that one's pupil can think of, is worth a try, provided that each experiment is given time. It will not be any good skipping from idea to idea without establishing a steady routine and allowing time for new practices to take effect. One thing is certain: for many dyslexics, sight-reading is usually hard work, but it is frequently the dyslexic who knows that they have to work extra hard to achieve their aims who is the most dedicated. If they find that they can actually enjoy sight-reading, all that dedication will have been worthwhile.

References

Associated Board of the Royal Schools of Music (2007) Guidelines for candidates with dyslexia or other learning difficulties, http://www.abrsm.org/exams/ specialNeeds/ (and then follow the links), accessed 17 July, 2007.

Frith, U. (1985) Beneath the surface of developmental dyslexia. In: J.C. Marshall, K.E. Patterson and M. Coltheart (eds), *Surface Dyslexia in Adults and Children*, Laurence Erlbaum, Brighton.

Cameo Three

Personal observations of dyslexic pupils in both literacy and music skills

Margaret Howlett-Jones

Eye movements: I've watched some pupils' eyes not moving in a direct line across the page. There is a jerky to-and-fro movement as though reading and re-reading. One sometimes has the impression that reading right to left would be preferable. I have also observed reading and spelling where the end of the word is dealt with first. This can result in hearing the last sound most clearly and create confusion in frequently used words.

Underlining words (probably also connected to eye movements above): the pupil, not always left-handed, most frequently underlines from right to left; so for 'truck', the first sound connected to the underlining is 'ck'.

Transpositions: these can be of words, syllables, notes or phrases, and must have some connection with the above.

Following on: that is reading on from one line to the next. Some pupils find this really difficult. This again refers back to eye movements and connects with the fact that slow readers are not anticipating the sequence of words/notes and therefore not 'searching' the sequel in the same way as able readers.

Inner turmoil (a very personal view!)

I believe that this comes about via the compensatory factors that dyslexics resort to in order to be seen to be equal to their peers. In the early years of schooling, the comparison of pupils' reading skills is well exposed, and feelings of inadequacy can set in. The more bright and forthright can develop means of covering up; some act the part of the capable reader but are not tracking at the correct speed. This becomes habitual and the reading becomes fault-ridden, with near-words, reversals and guesses from the initial letter noticeable. It reminds one of the camouflage tactic employed when the pupil is 'fed up with sight-reading this piece every lesson' and attempts to memorise the piece to avoid that.

In a calm one-to-one situation and with the use of a metronome, it is possible to slow the reading, keeping a constant flow, at a pace where the pupil achieves greater accuracy. The panic is not evident and an honest, unhurried version is provided. This is a helpful line of action for the pupil to embrace; indeed, it may be a life-long tactic, especially when reading instructions, or in a timed test where special considerations cannot be organised.

I can think of piano pupils who had the above reading faults for the same reason. The metronome was invaluable.

It is advisable:

- *not* to remark, in the pupil's hearing, on differences between the special-needs pupil and their colleagues, as the difference may be construed as criticism
- to use the term 'tidying up': this indicates that there is a bedrock of inescapables in music-reading which need to be accepted, but that, little by little, the incorrect can be dealt with
- to use 'well done' (spoken with degrees of enthusiasm and surprise at times!): it is essential to the learner's self-esteem; successes should be noted and charted
- to pursue a 'keep moving' approach: many dyslexic children find a purely academic set of exercises a turn-off, but an exercise turned into a game is infinitely more memorable and successful in operation; therefore, hunting, pairing, fitting shapes, saying out loud with chants, singing, miming and more can be applied
- to apply a light touch: as above, responding to a dire piece of playing/writing with a gentle joke often allows a businesslike attempt to improve that section.

The 'no assumptions made' department

Do not assume that concepts like high and low have been taken on board by dyslexics. The same applies to comparisons. Just because a dyslexic knows the word 'down' (which they may first have noticed through dog vocabulary), it does not follow that they know that 'town' has the same sound-ending, similarly with musical patterns, sequences and intervals.

It can be a painstaking procedure, with the sound needing to be heard, with the saying of the word, felt by the mouth, seen and written in the best multisensory way.

Similarly, some fail to see the likeness of intervals and phrases in music. The aural impression is usually the strongest, so that, when notation needs to be attended to:

- listening, singing, playing
- comparing with like shape in the (perhaps enlarged) manuscript
- highlighting the repeat of patterns etc.

can be the answer.

And the 'minor triumphs' department

Amy (7+) at a recorder class:

'You mean to say that every time I see a note on the middle line, it's B with one finger – *every* time?'

The combination of requirements, the dependability of the music notation system and pleasure at discovery are filtering across to this non-reader's music!

eleven

Sight-reading and memory

Michael Lea

In this chapter, I offer some thoughts arising from dyslexia research on why I could only memorise on one instrument, the guitar, and only sight-read on another, the cello.

Listening to music is self-evidently an aural process. For the performer, music is a tactile as well as an aural process. Music to the performer has a sound and a feel. I think of music in part as a structure, with time added to the space, music being multi-dimensional and multi-stranded. It is a structure to be physically and mentally explored, understood and created.

In Western classical music, there are usually two parts to the production of music: the composer who creates the piece and writes down the notes and the performer who interprets and performs the notes, bringing to the role their own interpretive insights and experience. Either or both roles surely must appeal to dyslexics of every type, with their ability to be comfortable with multi-spatial thoughts and actions.

As a professional classical double bass player, I have long prided myself on my sight-reading ability. This ability enables me not only to play the notes but also to perform at sight while playing in many different styles. This natural ability first surfaced when I was a chorister at Salisbury Cathedral. In those days we sang eight services a week, 44 weeks a year, with little repetition of music.

In contrast to my sight-reading skills, my natural memorising skills are poor. I have, though, in recent years acquired an expertise in memorising. While I can now memorise with confidence, it is still only the result of a great deal of focused effort. In order to memorise a piece, I relearn a piece again from the beginning without music, having first learnt the piece with music. For me, learning to play a piece and memorising a piece are two separate processes.

I can remember, aged 10, thinking there must be some trick to memorising. I resolved to make sure that one day I would find out that trick. At school I had had great difficulty memorising anything, such as spellings, vocabulary, names and dates. My writing was an illegible scrawl with many crossings out. I learnt much later that I was dyslexic. I wish I had known when young that sounding out loud what I needed to remember works. I wish I had known then that this works even better if you write at the same time as sounding out loud.

It is known that dyslexics may be poor at reading musical notation and may be poor at memorising music. However, the particular difficulties that an individual dyslexic can have vary widely from individual to individual, often with paradoxical effects. *Music and Dyslexia: Opening New Doors*, edited by Miles and Westcombe (2001), provides evidence of these effects.

Back in 1965 I was studying the cello and the guitar at the Guildhall School of Music. This was before I switched to playing the double bass. It came as a big surprise to me to find that on the guitar I was very poor at sight-reading and good at memorising. This puzzled me as I had long felt disadvantaged because of my lack of memorising skills on all other instruments.

At that time I could easily read music, but my playing skills on the cello were not advanced enough to be able to play everything I could read. Of the passages I found difficult, some I was not able to play at all. Others, less difficult, I found a way around, making the effect any way I could. In the easiest passages I was able to relax while playing and think of the sound, technique or matters of musical and ensemble interest. As my playing skills increased and more passages became easy, I was able to add in more musical and ensemble interest while playing at sight.

On the guitar everything was complicated and new. The movements involved when playing the guitar centre on the fingers. This co-ordination between the fingers of each hand is complex. My teacher taught me to practise with a metronome going at the speed at which everything worked comfortably. This might be very slow indeed. If there was any hesitation, then the metronome would be put on even slower. Every fingering was precisely worked out in both hands. For the right hand, which plucked the strings, I was taught to say out loud which finger was being used, particularly when playing scales and similar exercises. To sight-read while doing all these things was clearly impossible, as every note had to be right before the next one could be played.

In contrast, on the cello, while I was learning technique in a similar way to the guitar, I could also lose myself in the sound and sensation of playing long bows on open strings. The neurological messages were perhaps more diffuse, involving complex movements in the arms, different parts of the bow as well as different parts of the string. The sweeps of the bow were a much freer way of playing than the guitar. I was, however, visually locked onto the music on the music stand. Without the music in view, I would panic and be lost, even while playing music I knew well.

I do not think it can be much of a surprise to anyone familiar with Orton–Gillingham techniques for teaching dyslexics literacy skills (Gillingham and Stillman, 1969) that my memory was being activated when playing the guitar. I was having to concentrate on every note in both hands. I was saying out loud what I needed to remember. I was building up my technique step by step. This was structured, multisensory learning. However, I do not think this in itself explains why I was unable to memorise on the cello and unable to sight-read on the guitar, for I was applying similar techniques to learning the cello.

It might be thought that, on the guitar, there is a reliance on muscle memory for rote learning where it is quite a complex task to convert marks on a stave to the right muscular movements. In contrast the movements when playing the bass, at least in the case of the right arm, the bowing arm, are relatively coarse and therefore not such a cognitive load when it comes to sight-reading, but as there is not so much fine-muscular memory involved, memorisation on the bass is more difficult.

Aural memory linked to muscle memory is a powerful combination that clearly aided my memorising skills on the guitar. The fingers in both hands are in direct contact with the strings; so the neurological connections are direct. It would be expected that harpists and guitarists might have a memory advantage here over string players using a bow. In support of this I observe that pop guitarists can be seen always performing from memory while the string players playing alongside them generally play from music.

However, while I think that there is greater scope for neurological confusion playing the bass, there being more moving parts, I would like to think that the sensitivities involved in playing a bass are as well developed as on any instrument. As a bass player I have reservations with the idea that bowing on the bass is relatively coarse. While this idea is perhaps understandable to some, given the seeming unwieldiness of a bass bow, I would suggest that the bow of every stringed instrument, when first learning to play, is relatively coarse compared with using the fingers directly, as when playing the guitar or harp. Additionally, it is the case that some bass players are good at memorising; so I do not think a lack of facility at memorising is linked to a particular instrument. I note too that muscular memory is important in playing an instrument,

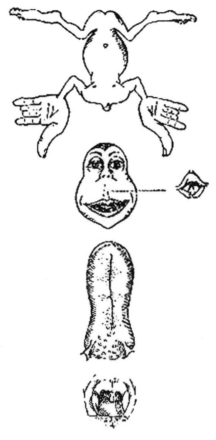

Figure 11.1. An illustration of a cortical homunculus. (Reproduced from O.L. Zangwill's *A Modern Introduction to Psychology*, published by Methuen & Co, London, p. 101.)

whether playing from music or from memory. I suggest therefore that it is necessary to look deeper into the processes of playing an instrument for an explanation of why I was able to memorise easily on the guitar and sight-read fluently on the bass.

The relative degree of cognitive load is perhaps significant. Looking at the diagram of a cortical homunculus (Figure 11.1), which shows the body in the proportions of its neurological input, the differing and large sizes of the fingers and thumbs immediately catch the eye, as does the small size of the arms. It is of interest too that there is a significant cognitive load in the shoulders, both hands and shoulders being important in playing a bass.

The large size of the thumb, followed by the lesser, but still significant, size of the first and fourth fingers, would seem to have all kinds of implications for playing the bass. For instance, the famous nineteenth-century virtuoso bass player Bottesini mainly used these fingers. From study of an original copy of Bottesini's *Complete Method for Double Bass*,[1] it can be seen that, in the half position, Bottesini played semitones using the fingers one and four and he extended the fingers one and four for tones. His use of the thumb enabled him to climb all over the highest reaches of the bass with ease.

If we look at Bottesini's own solo music, which is designed to be played in public from memory, we see that he never replays any repetitions in the music in the same way. Even when the notes might be the same in separate passages, he has a different phrasing or bowing to differentiate the passages. This means that in the pressure of performance he always knew where he was and could never find himself on a memory loop. I suggest that Bottesini was thus exploiting his neurological strengths to maximise his memory.

I would add that until printed sheet music was widely available in recent times pupils had to copy out what they wished to study before they were able to start to play it. Bottesini went further and composed his own music to suit, and develop, his own playing. I think there might be implications here for modern classical playing in comparison with pop musicians, who do compose and copy, and are I suggest as a result focused and direct. I note again that pop musicians are always seen performing what are often highly programmed and complex pieces without music.

These thoughts are still all to do with playing, whether improvising, memorising or sight-reading. I suggest that it is necessary to continue to look further for an explanation of the differing abilities to sight-read or memorise on different instruments.

Consider the concept of the hare and the tortoise, often used to describe different types of dyslexia. The hare tears along, covering the ground lightly, seeing an overview of the terrain and adjusting at speed. The tortoise, whose mind can be working just as fast, travels slowly, examining every blade of grass and every minor variation in the ground. The hare might well see different features every time he goes past, making memorising of detail difficult, while the view of the tortoise, being comprehensive, is much more consistent, allowing detail to be easily

---

[1] Bottesini, G. *Complete Method for Double Bass.* The original edition in English, rare and out of print, shows Bottesini's own fingering system. Modern editions, while keeping the notes, have the fingerings changed to those of the editors.

memorised. The hare does remember all kinds of things about the piece and is able to see all kinds of connections, but the process of being able to play the piece from memory might be difficult. This analogy seems to me to work well with musicians, the hare picking out the notes he needs to land on to keep going and the tortoise covering every note exhaustively.

On the guitar, I was a tortoise. I never achieved the lift-off of the hare. On the guitar, I was methodically playing in time to a metronome. The detailed messages that I was receiving were all clearly and closely defined. In addition, my amazement at being able to memorise made me relaxed about memorising, which in itself helped. These factors aided memory.

Referring back to the diagram of the cortical homunculus, I note the size of the eyes. Could the eyes be in some way a negative influence hindering memorising? I am told it is the case that blind people find their other senses have quickened as blindness progresses. In order to memorise, I have to put away the music and feel my way through a piece completely afresh, as though blind. This perhaps centres my thoughts back onto my fingers in a more intense and different way than when playing from music. I become intensely aware of the feel and position of my fingers on the strings and the hair of the bow on the strings. Allying this strong feel with the sound that emerges and the musical demands being made perhaps reinforces the neurological message aiding memory.

A less-well-known use of the eyes is the use made of sight by people with a deteriorating sense of balance, perhaps as a result of neurological deterioration, as in multiple sclerosis. As well as using their hands to lightly touch something so that balance can be achieved rather than their weight supported, they might use their eyes to 'hold onto' a wall. They are using their sight to maintain balance and can have difficulties standing upright with their eyes closed or in the dark. Isn't this similar in some way to the musician who is 'lost' without the music in front of them, even when playing music which has long been familiar to them?

I suggest too that a further understanding of the use of the eyes might be found that also links in with dyslexia, for isn't there a connection with the visual short-term memory, a memory that is typically weak in dyslexics? Orton–Gillingham techniques (Gillingham and Stillman, 1969) for teaching literacy skills are aimed at directly accessing the long-term memory. An example is learning a letter. The teacher writes a large letter filling a single sheet of paper. If, for example, the letter is A, the teacher says out loud the name of the letter, an example of the letter and the sound of the letter – 'A, Apple, a' – at the same time as writing the letter. The pupil, using a different coloured crayon each time, copies over the letter saying the same words in the same sequence. Finally, the pupil

97

closes their eyes and writes the same letter. The pupil's blindfold version will follow closely the line of the previous versions. The motor memory is established, linked to the sight and sound of the letter. The difference in emphasis and feel can be experienced by writing a letter in the air, first with the eyes open and then with the eyes closed.

When learning the cello, I was trying to create immediacy between seeing a note on the page, making the appropriate movements and hearing the sound. This is something of the same effect as a typist copying a letter with creative and interpretive elements added in. The typist is typing by feel while looking at a separate piece of paper. On the cello, my eyes were fixed on the music looking for the tiniest clues; my ears were fixed on what I was playing and what was happening around me. Thus, a circle was created in which memory of the printed music need play little part. Neither was I looking at where I was playing on the instrument.

On the guitar, I was looking at the music and my fingers. Guitar fingering and hand shapes being complicated, perhaps looking at the fingers and thus involving the eyes, as well as linking the actions with the sounds, completed the memory circle. The printed music was soon dispensed with.

Thus, my suggested explanation is that there is a general approach to playing that accesses in some way completely different and separate thought processes, enabling sight-reading skills to predominate. Similarly, I suggest that there are distinct and separate thought processes for memorising skills. I suggest that the differing uses of the eyes are important to each approach.

In my case I was forced into memorising by the particular demands of playing the guitar, while on the cello my aim was to learn to play the music from the printed notes as fluently as possible. Before studying the guitar, I simply did not know that it was possible to access my memory, as a result of not knowing the technique of how to do so and not having the confidence to know it was possible. It was completely outside my experience. My compensating skill on the cello was that I developed my sight-reading.

To illustrate this further, when in conversation with musicians who have a photographic memory, it is striking to me that they describe remembering the page as though they are experiencing every detail of it in the same way as experiencing being in a room. Thus, instead of noticing the position of the furniture as they would if in a room, they remember the physical nature of the paper, the print, the position of the staples etc. I suggest it is their experiential memory that is being activated. They are in a sense inside the print and the paper.

Thus, is understanding the differing uses of the eyes in relation to the experiential memory the key? Is it this that helps determine whether the player is naturally a tortoise or a hare on their instrument with the corresponding implications for memorising and sight-reading? Can the neurological balance be tipped in one way or other by the varying use of the eyes, either as a result of the demands of the instrument or as part of the particular make-up of the individual, or both? I suggest it is, and, yes, it can be. Certainly, I learn first to play a piece with the music in front of me. Then, I put away the music and learn the piece again from the beginning from memory. Finally, I learn the piece a third time concentrating on performance and musical matters. I am then ready to perform in public with, or without, music, solos without music, ensemble playing with music.

I hope I have provided information that is helpful to others who might be interested to take these thoughts further and perhaps in different directions and for those musicians wishing to develop their sight-reading or memorising skills. I hope too that non-musicians looking at dyslexic traits in these situations, outside their personal experience and involvement, may be helped in their understanding of dyslexia, with its varying difficulties and compensating advantages.

For me, learning to memorise has brought additional confidence to my playing in the orchestra, particularly in exposed or solo passages. Accessing the different processes involved in memorising has added an extra dimension to my playing, as does just knowing what it feels like to play from memory. Studying dyslexic learning techniques has given me ideas that I would not otherwise have had, and reinforced what I had found worked using trial and error. I now know that I can memorise if I wish to, an option that I did not have at all when young.

References

Gillingham, A. and Stillman, B.E. (1969) *Remedial Training for Children with Specific Difficulty in Reading, Spelling, and Penmanship*, Educators Publishing Service, Cambridge, MA.

Miles, T.R. and Westcombe, J. (eds) (2001) *Music and Dyslexia: Opening New Doors*, Whurr, London.

twelve

Ten top tips and thoughts

Nigel Clarke

1. Find out what you are good at and work hard to develop that skill. Don't let others knock you off course. Life is not a race: it's the end product that counts.
2. Be open about your problem/learning difficulty. You will find that people are generally helpful and understanding.
3. Learn to laugh at yourself. Rather than being resentful that you can't do things, be positive about what you can do.
4. Find out the policy on dyslexia/learning difficulties in the company/institution that you work for/study within.
5. Seek out role models that have the same challenges as you, for example Sir Winston Churchill, who was an educational disaster but ended up with the Nobel Prize for Literature.
6. Find someone you can trust who can check your written work.
7. Hard work and preparation are a great form of defence. Much of what you do can often be done away from the gaze of others.
8. Regard what you do as an asset and advantage. It's why you are unique!
9. Become a master of your computer spelling and grammar checkers or expert in a music-printing programme.
10. Remember there will be a lot you can do that others cannot!

thirteen

Can computers help? Matching the inner with the outer ear

Adam Apostoli

Today, whether we like it or not, technology surrounds us wherever we are. In fact, the world as we know it would come to a complete standstill without the assistance of technology. So with all this technology in the world, how is the dyslexic who chooses to make music affected or even helped by it? I am a student at the University of Edinburgh in the third year of a four-year degree programme in music technology. I am also dyslexic. In this brief chapter I will discuss how technology regularly assists me in performing traditional tasks like composing and editing music, how I use technology creatively and the challenges this presents.

Creating scores with Sibelius

Ever since Sibelius first released its music notation software, Sibelius 7 in 1993, the relationship between music and technology has grown. I first came across Sibelius while at school in 1999, when it was installed on two computers in the music technology suite. It was introduced to me at the time as a sort of music word processor, to be used when I'd finished my composition, written it out and wanted to make it look more professional. Now don't get me wrong, printed Sibelius scores look much better than handwritten manuscripts (well, mine in particular). However, I quickly learnt that Sibelius was not just a 'music processor', but an extremely useful tool, soon to be an integral part of my creative process. As a dyslexic, I found one of the most difficult and infuriating tasks I faced was converting musical thoughts and ideas into a paper score that even vaguely represented the music I heard in my head. Sibelius really helped me overcome this by providing an in-built playback facility which played back my score (albeit using crude MIDI[1] instruments) while having a cursor that moved along, highlighting the notes being played (not too dissimilar from karaoke really).

The ability to actually hear the score before other people play it and to have the knowledge that what you've written is exactly what you intended is immeasurably useful. Sibelius obviates the need for endless drafts, because when something doesn't sound right it can easily be altered. I remember having to copy out a song for voice and piano accompaniment. I rewrote it several times because I'd made holes in the paper with the number of corrections I'd had to make. Redrafting was a ridiculously long and laborious process, but there was no other option; it was either redrafting or my work was a mess, due in no small part to illegible handwriting. As I began using Sibelius, I found myself using it more and more frequently, not only for copying out my compositions but also for creating them. I would have never written any of the pieces I did for symphony orchestra without the help of Sibelius; the ability to hear the individual lines really helped to build up the composition into the music I heard in my head.

On another note, I revise both my compositions and editions constantly. Using Sibelius helped me get over the frustration of producing untidy scores. It also helped me by providing support during the creative process and by allowing me to not become distracted by the state of my score, instead letting me continue and create, doing the necessary formatting automatically along the way. Without this support, my compositional and editorial output would have been severely reduced, as I would have inevitably spent a great deal of time rewriting my work, becoming annoyed and stressed before eventually losing interest entirely.

---

[1] MIDI stands for Musical Instrument Digital Interface. MIDI is a digital data format that does not contain music but 'event messages' like pitch, duration, volume, tempo and vibrato, to name a few. MIDI is an agreed standard maintained by the MIDI Manufacturers Association.

Samples: the personal orchestra

As I stated earlier, Sibelius can play back the score I have realised using crude MIDI instruments, but due to sampling technology it is also able to produce a more lifelike rendition. Sample technology, for those who don't know, is a method of synthesising using short recordings of sound from real instruments (samples) playing one note. The synthesiser then processes these samples so that the original sample of a single note is converted into a playable scale. Never mind the mechanics of sampling technology, does it really matter how lifelike the instruments sound? Well, in short, yes. When you create music and play it back using the default MIDI sounds on your computer, it doesn't matter how detached you try to be from the sounds, you do actually make creative decisions based on what you hear. For example, some specific writing for string instruments may sound great in concert but when played using these default MIDI sounds this writing may not have the same effect. This may lead you to question when you're composing whether or not this technique actually works. Good samples are no replacement for a full orchestra or, indeed, any live ensemble, but they do bridge the considerable gulf between live and MIDI performance, and are certainly useful when constructing music.

I find that, when composing, using a good sampler and hearing my work build and grow with a degree of realism is extremely useful. I find it informs my writing and better matches what I hear in my head, subsequently sparking off new ideas that develop further.

Sonic art and computer composition

Sonic art and composition without the need for musical notation could be seen as a dyslexic's dream, as it cuts out the translation barrier and allows the musician to communicate directly with the audience, working exclusively with the sound. I find that when I write music I don't readily think in notes; I actually think in sounds, colours and textures; so inevitably when I translate my ideas into musical notation I quite often lose some sense of what was originally intended. The two highly popular music-sequencing programs I use for working with sound are Apple's

Logic Pro and Digidesign's Pro Tools. These are two of the many industry standard audio-editing applications used by a vast number of people who work with sound. I find that, when I create a composition, my creative process is not structured, which lends itself to using sound rather than producing a score. The flexibility, fluidity and precision with which I can work with sound leaves me not with a compromise but, most of the time at least, with exactly the music I intended. This music never has to be translated by musicians later on, as it's recorded and played as music in its own right.

> I dream of instruments obedient to my thought and which with their contribution of a whole new world of unsuspected sounds, will lend themselves to the exigencies of my inner rhythm.
>
> Edgard Varèse (1883–1965)

Another way I use music technology in creating music is by designing new digital instruments. In designing these instruments, part of the process includes designing the interfaces[2] used to control them. I use Cycling74's Max/MSP to do this. Using this program, any instrument or musical device can be created and controlled with any control surface that produces a recognised output (for example a computer mouse, a digital writing tablet, even a Nintendo Wii controller). In using this program, it really is possible to create instruments that are obedient to the musician's thought, thus uniting the inner and outer ear. However, when creating these instruments, the issue of a usable interface to control them is one that arises frequently. A difficult and fiddly interface makes the creation and development of music extremely difficult. I have found that the best interfaces are the ones that are the most intuitive, and that being dyslexic helps me in designing such an interface.

Technology as a hindrance?

So far I have sung the praises of technology and its use in music. I am also sorry to say that, although technology may do wonderful things, there is very seldom an occasion when it just works. Far too many hours have been spent tweaking software, finding out how to do something on the

[2] An interface is usually the set of controls and means with which a user interacts with a program on a computer. It encapsulates the look and feel of a program.

computer that would take seconds by hand and reading through large and complicated manuals before even beginning to work.

Something else I have found which renders technology a hindrance in music is the incompatibility between different software and hardware solutions for dyslexic musicians. The situation becomes so bad on occasion that I have been known to walk round with two laptops and other hardware peripherals just to transcribe a single lute tablature. I have found that, if technology doesn't integrate easily into your life and instead you end up with many different components doing different things that could be integrated into one solution, technology not only hinders mobility but also singles out its users and draws unnecessary attention to them. Furthermore, this technology is not only expensive to purchase in the first place but also requires expensive upgrades fairly frequently.

Technology and the future

For the dyslexic musician like me, technology in music not only makes traditional tasks bearable but also keeps the creative spark alive, allowing creative expression without the need to worry about the way a score is written or how legible it is. The ability to play back what has been written is also a brilliant feature of technology, and, with the advent of more lifelike samples, this means that the gap between what is heard in the inner and outer ears is brought ever closer. If it weren't for technology in music, and particularly Sibelius in my case, then my compositional interest would have died off a long time ago.

Technology in music, however, not only assists the dyslexic musician with traditional tasks but also opens up completely new fields, for example computer music and composition. This new composition, which relies solely on sound and technology rather than the translation of ideas into notation, provides dyslexic musicians with the ability to express themselves neither with limits nor with the feeling that they need to compromise on a score. Technology has certainly helped me over the years and continues to do so. The only aspect I would like to see improved is that it becomes more affordable and more integrated, so that the gap not only between the inner and outer ears but also between the dyslexic and non-dyslexic musician is bridged.

Strategies and successes

fourteen

Positive connections across the generations

Annemarie Sand and John Westcombe

Introduction

It is a great misfortune that relatively few colleagues now in the music education profession are able to benefit from Margaret (Peggy) Hubicki's wisdom. For many years, she was a distinguished professor at the Royal Academy of Music (RAM). She devised a complete method for learning the stave (Colour Staff, fully explained in Miles and Westcombe, 2001) and surprised many by the quality of her compositions, fortunately recorded just before she died in early 2006.

Some of her wise teaching methods are hinted at by, and clearly had an effect on, Annemarie Sand, a Danish student there who came to be both receiver and passer-on of the precepts below. Three voices are heard in the course of this chapter – denoted by the initials AS (Annemarie Sand), PH (Peggy Hubicki) and JW (John Westcombe) – which begins by discussing the teaching strategies of Peggy Hubicki and then goes on to describe a student's entry to a music conservatoire and her rescuing a much younger colleague (Peter Haddon) in danger of failing his undergraduate course.

Teaching: from theory to practice (JW)

In the first part of this chapter, John Westcombe sets out some of the precepts that were the basis of much of Peggy Hubicki's learning and teaching strategies.

They began with:

Aims

- breaking facts into nameable sectors
- separation of details and clear focus on any problem

Facts

PH felt very strongly that *both* teacher and learner have knowledge, information and experience. Flexibility and understanding are crucial so that the teacher can work out how the student thinks in order to help find new ways for the student to learn. They share common ground!

There are both differences and similarities between the student and their teacher. Dyslexics can become confused and lost in a fog for many reasons and need much support from those around them, at home, at school, friends. These supporters need unlimited patience and the ability to feel what it is like to be in their pupils' shoes, sharing the viewpoint of unexpected difficulties and frustrations.

When the dyslexic student is trying to learn something they don't understand, it is very helpful if the teacher can:

- make the student feel that both are discovering it together, rather than if the student sits alone feeling that here is something difficult which they, for some reason, will find hard
- give clues and guidelines which help the student along the right path (without giving the solution itself). This can remove fears of being behind closed doors and the sense of feeling a fool.

Observations

Written music is a drawing. Its symbols represent:

- pitch (high/low), therefore different notes
- time (lengths of notes and rhythmic patterns) from which pulse and beat must be divined and felt in the body. The eye follows pitch symbols (up/down) and time symbols, which denote length (left/right). The eye sees detail on the page and recognises patterns. Instructions are sent to manipulate keys on the instrument and control vocal sounds.

The ear hears sounds of different pitches and volume, which can be gentle or menacing, everyday or for special moments. The touch and feel of an instrument and its tactile aspect are often forgotten. The finger feels what the eye sees and the brain recognises.

Useful points

Question to learner: What do you see, hear, feel?

By careful teacher-guidance and a many-angled approach, the student becomes aware of points of learning and grasping matter, to be locked in their brain at the same time.

Finding the right words in response may be difficult, not least through different meanings, spellings and relationships (and, for musicians, directions in different languages). Here it is important to try to think how the students think and would identify with the meaning, then find words which they understand and which make sense in their world right now. In this way, you establish common vocabulary and can then go on to encourage hand signs and body movement (make a great stave on the floor and leap the intervals or devise a musical hopscotch).

Separately, the learner may have difficulty in explaining a problem. Here again, the teacher needs to choose words carefully, from the student's vocabulary, that can relate to the problem in an imaginative way. It ought then to be easier to respond to the precise nature of the problem when the pupil says: 'I'm stuck!' The wise teacher can find out whether the difficulty is manipulative. You are on familiar territory and can then travel together through the music, discovering what it can consist of and learn as much as the student can manage in that lesson. Next time, continue the process, adding to the layers. Explaining this in a non-musical context might help:

Example

A pupil is late for a singing lesson and could not follow directions from the station to the teacher's house because the words on the direction signs meant little to him. He made telephone contact and the teacher changed tack to the visual surroundings: 'Can you see the church?' (As opposed to, 'Take the third left.')

The outcome of this little cameo is that, as opposed to feeling a failure, the pupil gains confidence, albeit over a small matter, and the teacher remembers to try more than one method of solving difficulties.

Many of these basics apply in later stages too.

Learning: from student to professional singer (AS)

Annemarie Sand, new to this country and to higher education, was fortunate to encounter Peggy soon after her arrival from Denmark. She relates the opening part of the story.

Peggy Hubicki helped me all my life as a musician, and as a person.

Before I went to RAM, Peggy worked with me for a year so that I would be able to pass the various music tests (in English) I had to pass to be eligible for the entrance examination. The education system in Denmark was quite well advanced in its attention to dyslexia, and there I was known in the system as dyslexic. Once here, I told no one. Much later, I did have a conversation about that. I had wanted to try to be normal and learn on a normal person's terms, not on 'handicapped' terms. I needed to feel free from people knowing, and by not telling I could find my own way of learning, and ultimately prove to myself, by succeeding, that I was as good as a non-dyslexic.

Peggy helped me contact a very experienced person who knew the singing teachers at the conservatoires at that time, and I took this person's advice, and am to this day still studying with that same teacher. Peggy also gave me moral support, total trust in my ability and, in helping me to achieve my goal in becoming an opera singer for real, helped me recognise what is needed for a singer to understand fundamental harmonic combinations and patterns, making the written music so much more accessible. Together we dissected problems, worked out what was wrong and found solutions, a process on which I continued to build for many years.

After Carsten, my son, was born, I valued these regular meetings highly. Peggy and I had amazing talks about what the bare essence is of what makes a musician. We decided to involve Carsten from early on (indeed pre-birth!) as a basic starting point – almost a colleague. We merged the kind of precepts outlined above with both his and my current thinking, developing reactions, competences and improvisation. I went to work right away, implementing the agreed basic structure, and with my own improvisation. Later, Carsten clearly also was able to put this systematic help into his schoolwork.

Over time this hands-on experience made a very big difference to how I looked at music and also to how I viewed the learning process. It made me:

- see and understand everything from a different angle
- isolate the basics of what's needed
- find out how to implant them in another person
- how that young person learns
- how the gradual building of every day's little contributions can bring surprising outcomes.

My own experiences as a professional singer and knowledge of how to learn were broadened; new ideas and ways appeared through interaction with other colleagues. Looking at problems, small and large, from two or three different angles has always been essential. Opera singers (and concerto players) cannot have their music with them on stage. The former might carry around with them a very brief summary of, for example, 'mood on stage, chorus action, love song at window, "Then it's me."'

Introducing Peter Haddon (JW)

John Westcombe explains how, and unexpectedly, Annemarie was approached to take on the formidable task of helping a student who had been failing. The precepts outlined above were fundamental to her plans.

Peter Haddon was identified as dyslexic when 13, while a senior chorister at Westminster Abbey, and won a choral scholarship to a strongly musical public school, where he also played bassoon and was a keen geographer and sportsman. He did not take music GCSE or A level, but he secured a coveted place at a music conservatoire with nine GCSEs and two A levels, and had good reason to assume that they felt that he could cope with the demands of the course.

All seemed to go reasonably well there, save that there was the occasional need to rewrite an essay. Serious problems arose when the college required a whole-year retake mid-course, entailing a recital, which he seriously failed through insufficient preparation. It was not that he didn't feel that he had to prepare; at that time, he had a serious problem with time management.

His confidence had been badly damaged by the failure. So, how were several new pieces of music in four or five different languages to be immaculately planned and prepared for the retake recital performance without error or sheet music? His parents despaired. Mrs Haddon, a divisional adviser for the British Dyslexia Association (BDA), sought high and low for a teacher, and by chance came upon a journal published by the BDA (*Dyslexia Contact*, vol. 23, no. 1, 2004) which had an article about Annemarie. The latter took on the challenge and takes the story on to its happy conclusion.

Successful teaching brings its own rewards (AS)

Peter Haddon is a very handsome, tall young man, with a beautiful bass-baritone voice, I later was to discover. He comes across as a very open person with great trust and kindness. I liked him, from our first professional contact.

He had come to me in the hope that I could help him pass an examination to be re-accepted for the last year of a four-year course at a music conservatoire.

First, we talked for two to three hours so I could get to know him as a person and also find out what problems his dyslexia was causing him. The next thing I did was to devise an ad-hoc programme for what he had to do between then and the examination. This comprised working on his music-learning and memory problems. We also concentrated on conveying dramatic meaning in a piece while ensuring that character was kept at the centre of his musical and dramatic interpretations.

We decided when to meet next, and I engaged Nick Bosworth, who is a wonderful and very experienced accompanist. He had very kindly agreed to play on the day of the recital examination also (an important factor in sustaining confidence for the rigours of the performance day and a highly recommended strategy for all to consider).

I think we met three times after this first meeting, and we would work for about two hours on the programme, which consisted of seven songs and arias in different languages. Every time we met, I would agree what his homework would be, between now and next time, and he would go away with great enthusiasm, doing exactly what we had agreed.

I was pleased that he worked so hard and impressed with his discipline and determination to succeed. I was also very happy about having managed to bring out facets of his technique and presentation that had obviously lain dormant.

At the end of our time together he told me that he had been amazed at how successful the process had been and was very complimentary. I felt quite sure that he could do it from the very beginning, but as a teacher you never really know until you have gone through the process.

Conclusion (JW)

Much as in the first pages of this chapter, Peggy Hubicki's firm teaching principles were identified; so, at this later stage, Annemarie's strategies are worth attention. She made him think about:

- preserving a firm rhythmic base
- counting out loud
- noticing features like descending scales
- having the phrase in his ear
- whether anything vital was going on on stage while he was waiting for his next entry
- learning ways to remain engaged with a piece even when he was resting between scenes
- analysing a piece from every angle (the dramatic, visual, musical, voice-control)
- and what, for example, it was that he had to do, apart from just singing the notes, to make this song German and this one French.

With some excellent mentoring and a determination to prepare well in all the demanding sections, this young musician approached the final recital of 45 minutes knowing that something special was required. Once again, Annemarie had been insightful and inspirational.

Soon afterwards, Peter Haddon had a recital report, which states:

What a glorious sound! alongside a Distinction, and marks for the language elements not far off. He now has a 2.1 Honours Degree, has quickly moved into the professional world instead of the impecunious student loan contingent which seemed almost inevitable at one stage. He has signed a contract with a much-sought-after small specialist choral ensemble.

Some of the fundamentals that Annemarie was imparting to her student, and still finding supportive in her professional life, were undoubtedly those which she herself had taken in at least a generation before. They are the basic precepts outlined in the opening of this chapter and echo the work she had done years before in promoting her son's musical development. Two typical traits of dyslexia – poor time management and poor organisation – had threatened Peter Haddon's future: the passing on of methods to improve these skills, as well as the support of his mother, was critical to this young musician's success.

Reference

Miles, T.R. and Westcombe, J. (eds) (2001) *Music and Dyslexia: Opening New Doors*, Whurr, London.

fifteen

Similarities and differences in the dyslexic voice

Paula Bishop-Liebler

A love of music unites all musicians, but they are also as diverse as the instruments they play and the type of music they enjoy. Dyslexic musicians, as a group, are no different: they often share similar strengths and difficulties, but also exhibit unique profiles which create diversity within their learning and support needs.

How dyslexia seems to affect individual musicians depends upon the interaction between a number of factors, including the person's cognitive profile and the severity of their dyslexia or dyspraxia, alongside practical considerations such as the type of music being studied, be it classical, musical theatre, pop or jazz, the demands of their course or career, for example whether or not they need to read music fluently, and the length and type of musical education they have received.

Commonly reported difficulties for dyslexic musicians include reading musical notation, especially sight-reading, learning new music quickly, rhythmic accuracy – especially from notation – memorising music, scanning music or following a conductor and then finding the right place in the score, sustained concentration and languages for singers.

When working with dyslexic musicians in a variety of conservatoire settings and in a variety of contexts (such as research, assessment and teaching), patterns of variety and cohesion are quickly seen. It is important to define the spectrum of similarity and diversity so that we can begin to understand more fully how dyslexia affects musical learning and how best to support these students. To illustrate this I will discuss the profiles of three dyslexic singers. I have chosen to focus upon singers to highlight the fact that within just one 'instrument', the voice, there is a great deal of variety as well as cohesion.

117

Singers are a diverse group, especially at the conservatoire level. One reason for this is that the voice matures later in life, which means that many singers come to musical training later than their instrumental counterparts and some may have had little or no prior musical training. This affects the learning profile of the student. For example, sight-singing may be difficult due to a lack of experience as well as possible processing difficulties associated with dyslexia. Singers also have the added difficulty of words to accompany the music. They will probably need to sing in a variety of languages which they may not have previously studied and may find challenging, owing to their dyslexia. These general and specific points need to be taken into consideration when working with a dyslexic singer, in order to develop appropriate strategies for them.

Fiona: Undergraduate classical singer

Fiona was diagnosed with mild dyslexia and dyspraxia on entering music college.

Musical background

She has been singing since childhood and has always had an interest in music. She plays the piano, although she finds it challenging. She followed a traditional music education at school before entering music college.

Fiona reported that she was having difficulty with the following aspects of her musical learning when she began her course:

- slow processing of both aural and written music
- co-ordination for conducting
- aural, especially dictation, and singing and clapping at the same time
- rhythm both aurally and from the score
- sight-singing

Music observations

Her primary concern was her rhythmical accuracy. She found it difficult to maintain a steady pulse accurately and did not 'feel' the strong and weak beats easily. She had some difficulty following musical scores accurately as she did not easily connect what she saw with what she heard, and sequencing the information was difficult.

Discussion

Fiona had a comprehensive musical education and it is therefore clear that her difficulties were not due to any lack of tuition but were likely to be related to her dyslexia and dyspraxia. One of the cognitive indicators of dyspraxia is difficulty sequencing and ordering patterns; this seems to have had a direct affect upon Fiona's musical learning, as pattern recognition, both aurally and visually, is an important aspect of musical processing. She also has poor short-term auditory memory, which makes it difficult for her to remember aurally presented materials.

When she learnt to connect her breathing with the rhythm, her voice quality clearly improved. She needed concrete strategies in order to process all the information on the score. Fiona had to process consciously a lot of the information which many singers process automatically, which slowed her processing down. With systematic learning strategies Fiona successfully completed her aural and conducting examinations and is now able to perceive rhythms more accurately.

Katie: Undergraduate jazz singer

Katie was in her mid-20s when she began her undergraduate course. She was diagnosed with dyslexia when she was at primary school and had received dyslexia tuition and extra time in examinations throughout her education. Owing to having been diagnosed early and having received appropriate support, Katie felt confident with her academic learning strategies. However, it was not until she went to music college and discussed her musical learning that she realised that some aspects of her musical learning which she found difficult might be connected with her dyslexia.

Musical background

Katie had studied music at GCSE and A level, although she found the academic elements challenging. She therefore decided to follow a more practical course and went on to successfully complete a music diploma with distinction. Katie had played the saxophone from an early age and began the flute while at secondary school. When she was 18, she decided to focus upon jazz singing.

She reported that she was having difficulty with the following aspects of musical learning at the beginning of her music college degree:

- musical harmony
- understanding and applying musical harmony to singing

Music observations

As Katie had opted for more practical music courses wherever possible, she had not fully developed her music-analysis and reading skills/strategies. Her lack of knowledge regarding harmonic language had not been a concern until entering music college, as she learnt music aurally. However, she now wanted to understand harmonic relationships in jazz in order to further her musical skills.

Discussion

Although she didn't need to read music fluently as she could learn music aurally, she did not feel confident that she knew about how music worked, and this affected her confidence in musical situations especially as she wanted to converse with other jazz musicians. Unlike classical singers, Katie did not have to deal with any difficulties she might have had with foreign languages as all her music was in English. As Katie had a history of difficulties with theory and notation, it was likely that these difficulties were at least partly due to her dyslexia as well as her lack of experience.

Lucy: Undergraduate classical singer

Lucy was diagnosed with dyslexia in her second year of an undergraduate degree. She came forward for assessment because she was having difficulties with French phonetics. Lucy had found strategies while at school to compensate for her difficulties with literacy; so it was only when she began to learn French phonetics, which highlighted many of the areas that Lucy found difficult, that she realised that she was finding it more difficult than her peers, which she couldn't explain.

Musical background

Lucy had followed a traditional music education at school, studying music at GCSE and A level. She studied the piano from the age of 10 to 16 and achieved Grade 6. She reported that she learnt most of the graded examination repertoire by ear; however, as the music became harder, this method became increasingly more difficult. Lucy had always enjoyed singing and when she left school she spent two years studying singing before beginning her undergraduate degree at music college.

Lucy reported that she was having difficulty with the following aspects of her musical learning:

- learning music quickly
- sight-singing
- rhythmical accuracy from the score
- learning foreign-language texts for songs
- phonetics

Music observations

As with many adults with dyslexia, Lucy had difficulty with accuracy and speed of processing in aspects of her learning; she could do each task separately, but it took her longer to process than her non-dyslexic peers. In her musical learning this was particularly evident as reading vocal music requires high levels of multi-tasking. Developing strategies to ensure that music was accurately learnt as quickly as possible consequently became the main priority for her dyslexia support.

Discussion

Through appropriate and timely support, Lucy developed many strategies to assist with her musical learning. In her dyslexia support sessions she developed a system for learning new music more quickly and thoroughly so she could make the most of each singing lesson or coaching as she was now properly prepared.

As part of these strategies for learning new music Lucy developed her language learning skills. These particularly focused on connecting the visual, motor and auditory aspects of language learning. When she began lessons, Lucy had difficulty distinguishing sounds accurately and so it was important to develop strategies to ensure that she could check whether or not each sound was correct. This was done in a number of stages, including systematically and consciously breaking down each word and connecting the sounds with their phonetic symbols. Although it took Lucy some time to learn the phonetic symbols initially, there are only a limited number of options. This meant that, once she had learnt them, she could be sure that she was pronouncing the words correctly. Lucy also used her strong kinaesthetic sense to learn the mouth shapes for each of the phonetic symbols, making the process much quicker. Having used these and other strategies, she was able to connect the phonetic sounds with the visual representation of the word and was able to read foreign languages more accurately without needing to check every sound.

Lucy also used technology to increase her independence in learning music. When given a difficult piece to learn, she would scan it into Sibelius, a computer package for writing music. Using this, she could hear and see the music simultaneously and manipulate the tempo. She found it particularly useful for checking her rhythmical accuracy.

These are just some of the strategies which Lucy developed in order to learn music quickly and accurately. One of the particular benefits of this was that Lucy became more independent and confident in her learning; she no longer had to rely upon friends and teachers to ensure that she had learnt her music correctly.

Conclusions

All three case studies demonstrate some of the diversity of learning profiles and priorities for support.

- The students' musical backgrounds created diversity (e.g. we would expect Katie, who had little experience in theoretical music, to find her course challenging due to learning new skills, but lack of prior musical training could not explain Fiona's difficulties).
- The nature and severity of the student's learning difficulty, be it dyslexia, dyspraxia or a combination of both, will in itself create particular learning challenges and priorities for support (e.g. in Fiona's case rhythm, in Lucy's languages and learning music more quickly and for Katie it was harmony).
- Studying music at a higher education level can in itself create new challenges for dyslexic musicians. The pressures of conservatoire

study, the large amount needing to be learnt, the accuracy of performance and, for classical singers, the need to learn music in many different languages can put pressure on the student's existing strategies. This can mean that even those who have developed effective strategies in the past often need to develop further strategies to maintain progress.

- Individual course requirements differ widely and consequently create different priorities for support. The realities of the career such as the amount of music needed to be learnt in a week will affect the strategies needed. All three students had difficulties with some aspect of reading musical notation and retaining aural information. However, in their different careers Lucy and Fiona were more likely to need fluent music reading skills than Katie, although she would benefit from the confidence which more fluent music reading and analytical skills would give her.

When teaching dyslexic musicians, as with all teaching, working with the student's strengths is imperative for success. In order to do this, I find it useful to spend time building up a detailed picture of the student's learning history, mapping the areas that the student currently finds easy and difficult, and identifying their preferred learning styles. This is followed by prioritising areas for initial development. As these students are usually already highly experienced musicians, the areas of difficulty are often subtle and complex. I therefore find that, with these students, the most effective dyslexia teaching is when it is approached as a partnership between the dyslexia tutor and student, where the dyslexia tutor provides the framework for discussion, as they can explain what dyslexia and dyspraxia are and how they often seem to affect musical learning, and the student can identify the specific ways they feel their dyslexia affects their learning and their performance with their particular instrument. By working explicitly as a partnership, rather than as teacher and student, the student can become an expert in their learning.

Having identified areas of difficulty and preferred learning styles, each task, such as rhythmical accuracy, needs to be broken down into its component parts so that strategies can be developed for each aspect using a multisensory framework. By explicitly identifying each process, the student can work on small targets and revise each step so that they grow in confidence and skill. This process of breaking down each task into manageable and explicit steps enables the student to take control of their learning and apply a systematic method to other tasks. This process is central to teaching students how to learn rather than what to learn.

sixteen

Thirty-seven oboists

Carolyn King

Introduction

In this chapter, I describe my experiences as an oboe teacher, and how I used the Bangor Dyslexia Test (BDT; Miles, 1997) as a screening test for dyslexia. Some of my pupils were dyslexic; some not. Brief sketches are given of a few individual pupils and attention is drawn to differences between those who are and those who are not dyslexic.

Dyslexia is thought to occur in up to 10% of the population, with around 4% being severely affected (Crisfield, 1996; Ellis, 1993, p. 94). This means that the instrumental teacher teaching, say, 50 to 100 pupils in a week might have five pupils with at least some degree of dyslexia. When I started teaching the oboe some 25 years ago, dyslexia was not a condition which was familiar to most music teachers, and was only acknowledged by class teachers principally concerned with teaching literacy. Music was definitely not a priority and the relevance of dyslexia in music reading and performing was probably not fully realised.

However, in the last 10 years dyslexia has become more openly acknowledged, to the extent that most schools and their music departments are now required to have a list to which teachers can refer of pupils with special needs. Such a list alerted me to the (previously unrecognised) fact that one of my pupils, who I had taught for some three years, was registered as dyslexic. This pupil (B6), who will be discussed in more detail later, had some problems with sight-reading and scales, which I realised could be due to her dyslexia, and I therefore decided to investigate how many others of my pupils were similarly affected. This investigation involved the screening of 37 oboe pupils for dyslexia using the BDT.

Dyslexia and oboe playing

Figure 16.1. The oboe. (Photograph of Howarth XL oboe by kind permission of T. W. Howarth and Co. Ltd, London.)

As has been excellently described by Sheila Oglethorpe (1996), dyslexic individuals can experience problems in many aspects of performing on most musical instruments. Reading the music – deciphering the significance of open or closed notes with tails going up or down, arranged on a mystifying set of five lines and spaces – is a major difficulty. This difficulty is compounded when two staves have to be read simultaneously, as when playing the piano. A hazy knowledge of left/right, up/down, high/low can cause all sorts of problems with learning the fingerings of most instruments. Co-ordination of the two hands, which on the piano and various other instruments may have to move in opposite directions, is likely to be made more difficult for pupils with a degree of dyslexia.

Playing the oboe is possibly one of the easier options for the dyslexic pupil. The oboe player only has to read one line of music. In addition, the instrument is positioned centrally, down the body's midline; the basic position of the hands does not move and the fingering system over-blows to the octave (rather than the twelfth, as on the clarinet), which means that a proportion of the notes have more or less the same fingering in different octaves.

Nevertheless, learning even the initial placement of the hands on the oboe can be troublesome for the dyslexic pupil, and although some of the fingerings will be familiar to pupils who have previously learnt the recorder, there are several which are crucially different and not particularly logical. In particular, the fingering for F natural involves *adding* a finger (the third finger of the right hand, which more usually covers the D hole) to the fingering for E (the normal sequence would be that adding a finger makes the note go lower). F natural is also one of the

125

few notes on the oboe for which there is an alternative fingering when it is preceded by certain notes such as D, E flat, C# or by low notes where the third finger (right hand) is already on the D hole.

The above examples demonstrate that, although the fingering is fairly logical, it is never going to be completely straightforward to play a scale on the oboe until the fingerings for the notes have been kinaesthetically programmed into the brain and fingers. This is especially the case for the dyslexic pupil, who may well have only a hazy idea of what the notes should be and who will not necessarily be helped by learning scales or pieces by looking at the music.

Testing for dyslexia

Having discovered that one of my pupils was officially dyslexic, it was necessary to determine how to screen all the others for dyslexia. An investigation of the tests available (and their feasibility for use during an oboe lesson) led me to the BDT.

This test, which was devised as a result of the pioneering observations of dyslexic subjects by Tim Miles during the 1970s, was first published in 1982. It provides a short (10- to 15-minute) screening test for dyslexia, which seemed ideal for use with oboe pupils within their individual lessons.

Miles' starting point in developing the BDT was that dyslexia equates with a particular 'pattern of difficulties'. His book *Dyslexia: The Pattern of Difficulties* (Miles, 1993) describes the development of the BDT from informal observations to formal screening test, with an explanation of the theoretical basis of the tests within the BDT.

In his book, Tim Miles came to the conclusion that the difficulties which dyslexic subjects experience with these questions can mostly be attributed to a difficulty with verbal labelling, which can also be described as a phonological weakness.

In other words, the BDT seems to be tapping into the fundamental difficulties which dyslexic subjects have; and although non-dyslexic subjects do have some problems with the test, it has been shown by Miles that there are significantly more 'dyslexia-positive' results in the dyslexic as opposed to the control individuals. It therefore seemed to me to be an appropriate screening test to conduct for the purposes of determining the degree of dyslexia which might be present within my group of 37 oboe pupils.

The tests in the BDT are summarised as:

(1) questions about left and right
(2) repetition of polysyllabic words
(3) subtraction
(4) recitation of mathematical tables
(5) and (6) saying the months of the year forwards and backwards
(7) and (8) repetition of an increasing series of numbers forwards and of a smaller series of numbers backwards
(9) questions about past or continuing confusion between the letters 'b' and 'd'
(10) questions about familial incidence of dyslexia or dyslexia-like tendencies.

Careful note was made of all hesitations when answering, or use of special strategies such as counting on fingers or turning round (when answering the left/right questions). The final scoring consisted of: dyslexia-positive responses (+), dyslexia-negative (–) or somewhere in between (zero). Two zero responses counted as one + (plus).

Having used the scoring method as detailed in the BDT booklet, the BDT index (maximum total possible 10) was found to range from zero to 7 pluses. Table 16.1 below shows the detailed BDT scores for all pupils, with answers to question 10 (familial incidence) in column 4.

Seven pupils had high BDT scores in the range of 5 to 7. When these scores are compared with those in Miles' list of known dyslexic cases (Miles, 1993, pp. 38–52), it can be seen that they clearly fall within the range of the dyslexia-positive group, with which Miles was dealing (all of whom were initially referred to him because of their reading and/or spelling difficulties). The high-scoring group of seven being studied here included four of my pupils who were known to be registered as dyslexic (B6, A7, F1, F2), one pupil who had not been diagnosed but showed many dyslexic traits (H1) and two pupils (A1 and D3) whose high score came as a complete surprise, as they did not at the time seem to have any serious musical problems and I was not aware of any reported difficulties with reading or spelling.

Within this group, four parents (B6, F1, D3, H1) reported diagnosed dyslexia in the family, two were not sure (A7 and F2, assigned a zero) and A1 was also doubtful (in retrospect should have been assigned a zero rather than a plus).

There were 18 pupils with low BDT scores of between 0 and 2. In this group, only two parents reported any evidence of dyslexia in the family.

Table 16.1. Detailed BDT scores for all pupils

Pupil ID	BDT score	BDT 1–10 scores	Familial incidence
		LOW	
F5	0.0	– – – – – – – – – –	No dyslexia
D4	0.0	– – – – – – – – – –	No dyslexia
A8	0.0	– – – – – – – – – –	No dyslexia
A3	0.5	0 – – – – – – – – –	No dyslexia
F4	0.5	– – – 0 – – – – – –	No dyslexia
A6	0.5	0 – – – – – – – – –	No dyslexia
D1	0.5	– – 0 – – – – – – –	No dyslexia
B14	1.0	0 – – 0 – – – – – –	No dyslexia
B12	1.0	– – – – – – + – – –	No dyslexia
G5	1.0	0 – – – – – – – 0 –	No dyslexia
E1	1.5	– – – – – 0 – – + –	No dyslexia
B3	1.5	0 – – – – – + – – –	No dyslexia
B5	1.5	– – 0 – – – – + – –	No dyslexia
C1	1.5	0 – – – – – – + – –	No dyslexia
B10	1.5	– – – – – 0 + – – –	No dyslexia
B8	2.0	– – – – – – – + – +	1st cousin dyslexic
A4	2.0	0 – – – – 0 – – – +	Paternal uncle dyslexic, mother not sure l/r
D2	2.0	+ – – – – – + – – –	No dyslexia
		MEDIUM	
A2	2.5	– – 0 + – – – – – +	Paternal aunt very poor speller, pupil A2 left-handed
B9	2.5	0 – – 0 – 0 – – – +	Maternal 1st cousin dyslexic
B7	2.5	0 – – – – – + + – –	No dyslexia
F3	2.5	– – – – – 0 + + – –	No dyslexia
B2	3.0	+ – – 0 – – – + 0 –	No dyslexia
B13	3.0	0 – – – – 0 + – – +	Mother very poor speller, maternal uncle very slow to learn to read
B11	3.0	0 – – 0 – – + + – –	No dyslexia
B1	3.5	+ – – 0 – – – + – +	Maternal aunt, maternal cousin, great aunt, paternal cousin dyslexic
B4	3.5	+ + – – – 0 + – – –	No dyslexia
E2	3.5	0 0 – – – – + + 0 –	No dyslexia
G2	4.5	+ 0 0 0 – – + + – nk	No reply
G6	4.5	+ 0 – + – – – – + +	Father probably dyslexic, 2 siblings probably mildly, pupil G6 dyspraxic
		HIGH	
B6	5.0	+ 0 0 0 – 0 – + – +	Paternal uncle, paternal 1st cousin dyslexic
A1	5.5	+ 0 0 0 0 – + + – +	Sister had spelling difficulties till 14, father similar
A7	5.5	+ – – 0 – 0 + + + 0	Mother has l/r problems, grandfather slow to read
F1	5.5	0 – – + – – + + + +	Mother dyslexic, grandfather probably
D3	5.5	+ – – 0 – 0 + + 0 +	Father dyslexic
H1	6.5	+ – + + + – – + 0 +	Paternal relatives with problems, father slow reader, cousins dyslexic
F2	7.0	+ – + + – 0 + + + 0	Neither parent good speller, no diagnosed problems

Note: l/r = left/right.

A group of 12 pupils had intermediate BDT scores from 2.5 to 4.5; within this group, five parents reported dyslexia or dyslexia-like traits within the family, although none of the pupils had any reported problems with literacy.

The musical abilities and problems of some of these pupils will be considered in more detail in the next section.

A selection of case studies

In this section I shall summarise the main problems which some of these 37 pupils had with the two aspects of oboe playing (scales and sight-reading) which seem to me to be most affected by the presence of a degree of dyslexia. Comments about both the sight-reading skills and scale-playing ability are mainly the result of personal observation of these pupils at the time of this study (2002) and in the ensuing years (to 2006). No formal study of scale playing was done, and, although more formal research into the rhythmic aspects of sight-reading did show a statistically significant positive correlation between rhythmic errors and an increasing BDT score (King, 2003, 2006), this did not always reflect overall sight-reading ability.

Good sight-reading seems to be the result of numerous factors, including the ability to look ahead (an eye–note span of 5–7 notes ahead is common in good sight-readers; Sloboda, 1985, Chapter Three), the familiarity of the musical idiom, memory of musical patterns and contour and establishment of a mental musical dictionary, auditory feedback and memory of what has just been played, recognition of phrasing and rhythmic structure and the ability to do multi-tasking (Lehmann and McArthur, 2002; Harris and Crozier, 2000).

The ability to play scales accurately and fluently also depends on many component skills, including a knowledge of key signatures, a technical facility with the fingers, especially with the very high notes, which are less frequently used, the ability to hear internally the pitch of the next note and to form the most appropriate embouchure and the ability to hear the pitch and access the fingering for the notes, especially when coming down the scale. Many of these aspects (theoretical knowledge, memory and sequencing, finger co-ordination) are likely to be problematic for the dyslexic pupil.

Table 16.2 below summarises all pupils' BDT scores, their ages and years of learning the oboe at the time of testing, with some comments

Table 16.2. BDT scores and comments about pupils' scale-playing and sight-reading abilities

Pupil ID	BDT score	Age when tested	Years learning	Comments about scales and sight-reading
	LOW			
F5	0.0	12.3	2.3	
D4	0.0	14.6	2.3	Scales and s/r very bad
A8	0.0	11.8	1.8	
A3	0.5	9.5	2.0	Scales and s/r very bad
F4	0.5	13.4	3.3	
A6	0.5	17.0	6.0	
D1	0.5	14.9	5.3	
B14	1.0	13.6	2.3	
B12	1.0	13.9	5.3	
G5	1.0	16.4	7.3	
E1	1.5	12.0	2.3	
B3	1.5	14.3	2.3	
B5	1.5	12.2	2.0	Scales and s/r bad
C1	1.5	9.3	1.0	Scales weak, s/r good
B10	1.5	9.3	0.8	
B8	2.0	15.1	4.3	
A4	2.0	8.8	1.0	
D2	2.0	14.9	3.3	
	MEDIUM			
A2	2.5	16.4	4.6	Scales and s/r very bad
B9	2.5	12.7	2.3	Scales and s/r very bad
B7	2.5	14.7	3.3	
F3	2.5	11.7	2.0	
B2	3.0	15.7	6.0	
B13	3.0	13.2	1.8	Scales good, s/r weak
B11	3.0	15.5	6.0	
B1	3.5	14.7	4.0	Scales very bad, s/r weak
B4	3.5	12.0	3.3	Scales and s/r very bad
E2	3.5	10.5	1.0	
G2	4.5	17.0	3.3	Scales and s/r very bad
G6	4.5	17.0	5.0	Scales and s/r weak
	HIGH			
B6	5.0	15.7	6.0	Scales very bad, s/r good
A1	5.5	14.7	2.3	Scales weak, s/r fair
A7	5.5	16.3	3.7	Scales and s/r very bad
D3	5.5	13.8	2.3	Scales weak, s/r good
F1	5.5	14.1	5.3	Scales and s/r very bad
H1	6.5	11.6	2.6	Scales very bad, s/r weak
F2	7.0	13.1	4.3	Scales very bad, s/r good

Note: s/r = sight-reading.

about scale and sight-reading ability. (Note: I have only specified scale playing as 'bad' or 'very bad' when I have found the pupil to have a real problem with scales, as distinct from problems resulting simply from a lack of practice.)

High BDT group (5–7)

This group of pupils with ages ranging from 11.6 to 16.3 years had been playing the oboe for between two and six years. There was one feature common to the playing of all of these pupils (except D3 and A1), which was their inability to play scales at their appropriate level, especially coming down. Perusal of their BDT results (see Table 16.1 above) shows dyslexia-positive (+) scores in Q8 (numbers reversed) in each case. It was noticeable that, even for pupils who could go up a scale successfully, turning round at the top and coming down was much more problematic, maybe because of the difficulties of remembering the sounds and accessing the names of the notes in reverse which had just been played going up. H1 was very bad at scales (see Table 16.2 above), and had noticeable difficulties in the recitation of mathematical tables section (question four) of the BDT as well as the number sequences (question eight).

The two pupils (D3 and A1) who had unexpectedly high BDT scores did not at the time seem to have serious problems with scales (both were at about the Grade 3 level). Subsequently, D3 has been referred for extra literacy help at school, and as he gets more advanced on the oboe he has found the scales very difficult. Pupil A1 has meanwhile given up, having got stuck at the Grade 5 level scales.

The sight-reading ability of this group of pupils was more varied. Very good sight-reading was a characteristic of pupils B6 and F2. Both of these pupils had been playing for several years, came from musically supportive families and had joined in lots of musical activities from an early age. B6 had also been a dancer for several years, which may have helped to embed good musical pitch and timing into her playing, as taught by Dalcroze (Pegg, 1994), and pupil F2 played the recorder from an early age. Both of these pupils had therefore had plenty of opportunities to absorb musical patterns and conventions and had been able to play alongside other competent players. Pupil F2's comments about her sight-reading ability were interesting. She said that she read music by 'letting her fingers do it' but would not necessarily know which notes she was playing.

By contrast, pupils F1 and A7 were both very poor sight-readers. A7 particularly had had very little musical support at school (where she was told she was stupid by her music teacher) or at home. She had never played in a group with other better sight-readers and had problems not just with rhythm but with identifying the notes. The stave appeared sometimes to have more than five lines – this was improved by the use of a green filter.

Pupils A1 and D3 seemed to be quite adequate sight-readers, and D3 continues to be a useful player in numerous groups. He also has a very supportive musical family.

H1, the youngest pupil of this group, had severe sequencing problems (very weak at maths) but had a very good ear and instinctive musical sense and was good at sight-reading music in an idiom with which he was familiar (from a choir-school background), but he was much less successful at most other kinds of music.

Medium BDT group (2.5–4.5)

This group of 12 'intermediate scorers' is interesting in a musical sense in that they frequently had problems with scales, which paralleled a difficulty with tables, or with musical memory, which was reflected in the digits forwards and reversed items of the BDT. Those who were bad at scales were generally not good sight-readers. None of these pupils was diagnosed as dyslexic from the literacy point of view; so some of the problems which were observed might be said to represent a musical variant of dyslexia, or 'formes frustes' (Critchley and Critchley, 1978), in which some but not all symptoms are apparent. It is interesting to note that of the seven pupils which I have noted as being poor at scales and/or sight-reading (A2, B9, B13, B1, B4, G2, G6), five had evidence of dyslexia in the family. Only B4 said there was no family history of dyslexia, and no answer was received from the parents of G2.

Unlike the high-scoring group, there were no consistent problems with questions seven and eight in the BDT. Pupil A2, for example, did well in these two tests but had problems with mathematical tables (in spite of being 16 years old) in which the answers require a memory of the total plus knowledge of where they are up to in the sequence ('six eights are 48' etc.). This pupil was very bad at scales and had been tested for dyslexia when he was 4 years old and shown to have some co-ordination and sequencing problems. However, he never had any literacy problems. This pupil was a very hesitant sight-reader even though he reached a high standard of playing (Grade 7) and coped by taking new pieces very slowly and methodically, and listening to CDs where possible. He always found playing in a group very difficult.

Pupil B9 did not read music at the start and was very slow to learn the notes. At the time I attributed this to a slight squint, which she said got worse when she was tired. Her eyesight was improved by remedial spectacles. This pupil had considerable problems with scales, which she could not remember and in which she often completely lost her way. This happened especially when she felt under stress, as was the case during her Grade 3 examination – which she passed but in which she failed the scales.

In the BDT she did quite badly on the tables (zero), some of which she found she could complete only if she said them as fast as possible. The same thing was true of her scales, which went well only if she could maintain the speed. This seems likely to be due to a very weak short-term memory – she regularly had to ask for things to be repeated and forgot which scale she was doing. Her singing teacher was of the opinion that she had 'auditory dyslexia'.

At the time of the original study, when this pupil was under 13 and had been playing for just over two years, she was not a good sight-reader. Since the original investigation, she persisted with the oboe and managed to take her Grade 5, in which she got a good pass, did well in the sight-reading but failed the scales. Another couple of years of reading and playing benefited her sight-reading, but her short-term memory did not really improve with age.

A few other pupils in this intermediate group had interesting partial manifestations of what I shall call 'musical dyslexia'. B13 worked hard at scales and usually did well with them but was a poor sight-reader even having taken her Grade 6 examination. Pupil B1 was very poor at maths and hopeless at scales but over the long time that she learnt the oboe her sight-reading improved a lot, although little things like tied notes would always throw her off track. She continued to learn the oboe (having played for about eight years) and managed to get to the Grade 8 level, although she still found playing in a group difficult. Pupil B4 apparently had no family history of dyslexia, but remained very poor at scales and sight-reading and seemed to have no internal pulse. She made very slow progress, even though she had been playing for over six years. However, she made a very good sound and had a very good sense of pitch.

Low BDT group 0–2

On the whole, pupils in this group reached acceptable standards of scale playing and sight-reading within the limits of how much practising they were able to do. However, there were a couple of notable exceptions.

Pupils D4 and A3 were both extremely bad at scales and sight-reading. D4 was a boarder at school, had no parental help and did not practise enough. He gave up after struggling at the Grade 2 level. At the time of writing, A3 still seems to have a genuine problem with scales, possibly owing to a weak short-term memory (similar to B9). However, she is still playing the oboe, has recently taken Grade 4 and her sight-reading is steadily improving as she gains more experience of playing in various groups.

There were two reports of dyslexia in these pupils' families (B8 and A4). However, B8 and A4 were both very good sight-readers and B8 especially was very good at scales; so the dyslexia syndrome does not seem to have been inherited here.

B5 and C1 are still not very good at scales (especially B5). Although I am not convinced that there is sufficient practice, in the case of B5 there seems to be a genuine difficulty that is clearly not related to a dyslexia problem.

Discussion

In this survey of 37 school-age oboe pupils, who were all screened for dyslexia using the BDT, it was interesting to find that four pupils had already been officially diagnosed as dyslexic. If the other three pupils in the high BDT range are included, the percentage figure is 19%. Considering that the generally accepted degree of dyslexia in the population is rekoned to be between 4% and 10%, this figure seems rather high, but is probably coincidental and the result of a fairly small sample size.

Of particular interest was the gradual emergence of a family history of dyslexia as increasingly dyslexia-positive answers were given to the other BDT questions. Of interest also were the individual characteristics (music- and sequencing-related) of the intermediate scorers on the BDT scale. It would be useful for the music teacher to be aware that some of the problems which were experienced by these pupils were similar in kind to those experienced by diagnosed dyslexic pupils who additionally have problems with reading and spelling.

It therefore seems likely that multisensory teaching strategies which are known to benefit the clearly dyslexic pupil (demonstrating rather than explaining technique, enlarging the music, playing scales rhythmically and fast, clapping and walking around the room to establish a pulse, singing, making more use of the memorising of musical sections) can also be helpful for pupils in the intermediate category. Similarly, any emphasis in the teaching process which makes use of the dyslexic pupil's often greater right-brain ability (the ability to appreciate phrases and melodic structure and the overall feel of the piece and to hear pitches internally) is going to be of benefit to dyslexic and intermediate pupils alike (Denckla, 1990; Platel *et al.*, 1997).

It is hoped that this report of the use of a fairly simple test for dyslexia will help other music teachers to make more sense of the bewildering variety of talents and difficulties which our dyslexic and non-dyslexic pupils demonstrate.

I would like to thank Professor Tim Miles for his advice and help with the interpretation of the Bangor Dyslexia Test.

References

Crisfield, J. (ed.) (1996) *The Dyslexia Handbook*, British Dyslexia Association, Reading.

Critchley, M. and Critchley, E.A. (1978) *Dyslexia Defined*, Heinemann, London.

Denckla, M.B. (1990) The paradox of the gifted/impaired child. In: *Music and Child Development*, F.R. Wilson and F.L. Roehmann (eds), MMB Music Inc., St Louis.

Ellis, A.W. (1993) *Reading, Writing and Dyslexia*, Psychology Press Ltd, Hove, East Sussex.

Harris, P. and Crozier, R. (2000) Teaching sight-reading. In: *The Music Teacher's Companion: A Practical Guide*, Associated Board of the Royal Schools of Music, London.

King, C.A. (2006) Dyslexia and sight-reading, *ISM Music Journal* **72**(February): 356–359.

King, C.A. (2003) *Music and Dyslexia*, MA dissertation, Chapter Three, University Library, Reading.

Lehmann, A.C. and McArthur, V. (2002) Sight-reading. In: *The Science and Psychology of Music Performance: Creative Strategies for Teaching and Learning*, R. Parncutt and G. McPherson (eds), Oxford University Press, Oxford.

Miles, T.R. (1997) *The Bangor Dyslexia Test*, Learning Development Aids, Wisbech, Cambridgeshire.

Miles, T.R. (1993) *Dyslexia: The Pattern of Difficulties* (2nd edn), Whurr, London.

Oglethorpe, S. (1996) *Instrumental Music for Dyslexics: A Teaching Handbook*, Whurr, London.

Pegg, L. (1994) The principles of influential music educators. In: *Principles and Processes of Music Teaching*, Music Teaching in Professional Practice (Mttp), International Centre for Research in Music Education, Reading.

Platel, H., Price, C., Baron, J-C., Wise, R. *et al.* (1997) The structural components of music perception: a functional anatomical study. *Brain: A Journal of Neurology* **120**(February, Part 2): 229–243.

Sloboda, J.A. (1985) *The Musical Mind: The Cognitive Psychology of Music*, Oxford University Press, Oxford.

seventeen

Suzuki benefits for children with dyslexia

Jenny Macmillan

Introduction

I believe many of the challenges encountered by children with dyslexia when learning a musical instrument are addressed by the Suzuki approach. Teaching programmes for people with dyslexia need to be structured, sequential, cumulative, thorough and multisensory. Plenty of listening to music, repetition of assignments, participating in group lessons, learning initially by ear and activities aimed at building pupils' self-confidence are recommended. The Suzuki programme covers all these issues.

The ability to play a musical instrument offers enjoyment and satisfaction, and raises self-esteem. However, learning to play an instrument requires concentration, co-ordination and memory, as well as auditory, motor and spatial skills – all areas in which people with dyslexia may encounter difficulties. Common problems faced by those with dyslexia when studying music include learning notation, sight-reading, melodic and rhythmic repetition and maintaining a steady beat.

I consider that many of these problems, identified in the research literature (Oglethorpe, 2002, 2003; Overy, 2000, 2003), are addressed by the Suzuki approach. Indeed, Shinichi Suzuki claimed his 'mother-tongue' approach to teaching children was effective for *all* children unless severely brain-damaged or disabled (Suzuki, 1982).

> There are no failures. Any child who can speak his native language
> has the potential to learn to play the piano. (Bigler and Lloyd-Watts,
> 1979, p. 2)

Rawson, writing in 1970, identifies the need for teaching programmes
for people with dyslexia to be 'structured, sequential, cumulative, and
thorough', as well as multisensory. With reference to learning music, the
British Dyslexia Association (1996) emphasises the need to build new
information on existing knowledge, while Westcombe (2001) stresses the
importance of providing plenty of opportunities to revise previous work.
Case studies of musicians with dyslexia by Backhouse (2001) and
Ganschow *et al.* (1994) mention the importance of repetition and of
listening to recordings when learning a new piece, the latter also claiming
that rhythms are easiest to learn by hearing them. The Suzuki programme
effectively covers all these issues.

The Suzuki approach is highly structured. Lessons often start when the
child is 3 or 4 years old, when children's aural and motor (though not
visual) skills are fully developed. Children begin by listening at length to
recordings of the music they will learn in their first few lessons. They also
listen to plenty of other good music so that the language of music
becomes familiar to them. As with learning any language, it is best to start
at an early age, and it is advantageous to be surrounded by the language
before and while learning it. Children spend some weeks observing the
lessons of other young pupils so that when they start their own lessons
the environment, the teacher and the expectations will be known and
understood by child and parent. Parents are greatly involved at this early
stage, creating a positive, nurturing home environment, surrounding
their child with music and observing lessons with their child.

From the very first lesson, posture and technique are emphasised as
much as the importance of learning to listen to one's sound at the
instrument. Teachers are careful to ensure that pupils start on suitably
small-sized instruments; young pianists need an adjustable stool and
footstool that allow them to sit comfortably with their feet firmly
supported and not dangling. Children work sequentially through a
common core repertoire of pieces, which gradually introduce and
develop various musical and technical skills. The repertoire progresses
from variations on *Twinkle, Twinkle, Little Star* through various folk songs,
minuets and sonatas to major works by the classical composers: Bach and
Mozart concertos on the violin, Haydn and Boccherini concertos on the
cello and Bach's *Italian Concerto* on the piano, for example.
Supplementary repertoire, including ensemble music, is often introduced
by teachers according to the needs of each student.

_____

The repertoire is carefully graded, each piece introducing one or two new techniques and otherwise building on the library of skills which the pupil is rapidly developing. The approach is thorough as pupils are required to master every musical and technical point in one piece before progressing to the next. Suzuki teachers give very specific instructions on how to practise to improve musicianship and technique. These instructions are demonstrated so the pupil can see and hear what is happening. The pupil will then be asked to repeat the exercise several times in the lesson so that the pupil, teacher and parent all know the pupil can achieve it. The parent notes down what is to be done and how, and encourages further repetitions at home. Dr Suzuki would ask pupils to practise an assignment many times, not so that they could play it correctly but so that they could not play it incorrectly (Suzuki, 1969).

The programme is cumulative as pupils are encouraged to maintain their past repertoire. Essential basic skills, such as listening to their sound and learning to produce a beautiful tone, as well as playing with accurate rhythm, balance and intonation, are improved mainly by working on review pieces, which are well known, rather than the newest, less-familiar piece.

Suzuki pupils learn using aural, visual and kinaesthetic senses. They continue to listen daily to recordings of the music they are learning. They observe other pupils' lessons before or after their own. They see their teacher demonstrate – they are asked to listen to the demonstration, to watch the hand and arm movements and may be invited to feel the movements by resting a hand on the teacher's hand. Because of the emphasis on technique from the very first lesson, they learn to be aware of every movement at their instrument; because of the emphasis on musicianship, they learn to listen very carefully to the sounds they are making. In the early stages, they learn by ear, removing the huge obstacle for many children with dyslexia of reading. Later, when learning music from the score, they continue to memorise very easily and normally perform from memory.

Suzuki children attend regular group lessons, in addition to their individual lessons, at which rhythm games and singing activity games are played. This type of activity is recommended by Overy (2000, 2003) following her studies of children with dyslexia. People with dyslexia have difficulty maintaining a steady beat (British Dyslexia Association, 1996). This can be helped by playing with other children in unison, duets or other ensembles at group lessons, as well as sometimes playing along with the recording as recommended by Suzuki teachers. Children learn well from their peers in groups, and there is the added benefit of the enjoyable social aspect of working together, developing musical skills in groups.

Music notation is generally taught to Suzuki children from their very first lesson in groups, through games with rhythm and pitch flash cards. Initially, Suzuki children play their instrument by ear. But once they have a secure technique and are producing a beautiful sound, they learn to read music while playing their instrument. Lauridsen (2002), a Danish piano teacher who has investigated using off-staff notation, traditional notation and no notation, considers that: 'not using any music notation at the beginning level may be a very effective method for developing important listening skills' (p. 14).

She thinks that advanced students are reluctant to engage in the process of elementary reading, and that they may find it difficult to unlearn the habit of looking at their hands when performing. In my experience it is a matter of carefully judging when to introduce reading skills at the instrument, having ensured that notation is learnt sequentially and thoroughly in group lessons. If reading is commenced at an appropriate time, Suzuki children have no particular problem in looking at the music and developing ear–eye–hand co-ordination, because their auditory and motor skills are so secure.

Indeed, Anderson (2006, p. 23, citing Odam, 1995) emphasises that:

'[R]eading music should never begin' until pupils are able to use and to manipulate 'musical sounds, procedures and constructions' fluently for themselves. [For those who] 'fear that pupils who learn initially by ear will never read as well as those who start reading notation in their earliest lessons . . . there is actually a growing body of evidence indicating that the reverse is true'.

Reading notation can be a huge difficulty for children with dyslexia. An approach which delays reading at the instrument until the aural and technical skills have been developed and allows independent, concentrated work on visual reading skills must be beneficial.

Backhouse (2001) mentions the low self-esteem that can easily develop in people with dyslexia. Typically, repeated scolding by unsympathetic teachers will destroy the child's self-confidence (Miles, 2001). Gilpin (2001), the mother of a cornet player with dyslexia, indicates that a structured approach with lots of repetition and praise is successful, and emphasises the importance of being well prepared for examinations. Suzuki teachers are trained to be very positive in their teaching and always to find something to praise before suggesting some aspect for improvement. They know it is essential for pupils to be thoroughly prepared for their regular concert performances, so that each performance is a good experience and builds self-confidence. As Suzuki children receive enormous parental support, especially in the early stages, they can start their lessons very young. While Suzuki children with dyslexia may be behind their peers in some aspects of their learning, they may well be in advance of non-Suzuki children in their music-making, and this helps build their self-esteem.

Plenty of listening to music, repetition of assignments, participating in group lessons, learning initially by ear and building self-confidence are to be recommended for children with dyslexia. These issues are all addressed by the Suzuki approach. Qualified Suzuki teachers have followed long and intensive training courses which cover child development and psychology as well as pedagogical and musical skills. They are, therefore, able to teach effectively according to each pupil's strengths by being flexible in their application of the Suzuki approach.

References

Anderson, S. (2006) Sound before symbol revisited: an alternative approach. *Piano Professional* **12**(September): 22–25.

Backhouse, G. (2001) A pianist's story. In: *Music and Dyslexia: Opening New Doors*, T.R. Miles and J. Westcombe (eds), Whurr, London.

Bigler, C.L. and Lloyd-Watts, V. (1979) *Studying Suzuki Piano: More than Music*, Summy-Birchard Inc., Secaucus, NJ.

British Dyslexia Association (1996) *Music and Dyslexia Information Sheet*, BDA, Reading.

Ganschow, L., Lloyd-Jones, J. and Miles, T.R. (1994) Dyslexia and musical notation, *Annals of Dyslexia* **44**: 185–202.

Gilpin, S. (2001) John and his cornet. In: *Music and Dyslexia: Opening New Doors*, T.R. Miles and J. Westcombe (eds), Whurr, London.

Lauridsen, B. (2002) Introducing music reading to beginners. *Piano Journal* **23**(68): 13–17.

Miles, T.R. (2001) The manifestations of dyslexia, its biological bases, and its effects on daily living. In: *Music and Dyslexia: Opening New Doors*, T.R. Miles and J. Westcombe (eds), Whurr, London.

Oglethorpe, S. (2003) Belief is the key: helping dyslexic pupils to succeed, *Piano Professional* **2**(April): 7–9.

Oglethorpe, S. (2002) *Instrumental Music for Dyslexics: A Teaching Handbook*, Whurr, London.

Overy, K. (2003) Dyslexia and Music: From timing deficits to musical intervention. *Annals of the New York Academy of Sciences* **999**(November): 497–505.

Overy, K. (2000) Dyslexia, temporal processing and music: the potential of music as an early learning aid for dyslexic children. *Psychology of Music* **28**(2): 218–229.

Rawson, M.B. (1970) The structure of English: the language to be learnt. *Bulletin of the Orton Society* **20**: 103–123.

Suzuki, S. (1982) *Where Love is Deep*, World-Wide Press, New Albany, IN.

Suzuki, S. (1969) *Nurtured by Love*, Senzay Publications, Athens, OH.

Westcombe, J. (2001) How dyslexia can affect musicians: In *Music and Dyslexia: Opening New Doors*, T.R. Miles and J. Westcombe (eds), Whurr, London.

eighteen

Dyslexia: no problem

Diana Ditchfield

Introduction

This chapter comprises two parts. In the first part Diana Ditchfield
reports on what happened during her meeting with Nigel Clarke; in the
second part she offers some personal comments.

A meeting between Diana and Nigel

When approached about contributing to this book, Nigel felt he had
explained his journey with dyslexia when writing a letter to his son,
Joshua, in a chapter entitled 'Silver lining' in our previous book (Miles
and Westcombe, 2001). He added that for him dyslexia was now no
problem. However, he was mindful that since dyslexia is of genetic origin
there was a possibility that his son might have inherited some of his own
difficulties. In this letter Nigel related his journey from failure to success,
particularly in the arena of musical composition.

Not much was known about dyslexia when Nigel was at school and he
could barely read and write when he was an adult. He joined the army as
a musician and embarked on a musical career, which was his preferred
choice and where his penchant and latent skills in composition were

fostered. This led eventually to a very successful studentship at the Royal Academy of Music.

Nigel said that his experiences in the army gave him time to catch up in literacy, and he paid extremely high tribute to Robin Page and to his wife, Liz. Neither they nor Nigel knew that Nigel was dyslexic but rather thought he was a late developer. They helped him with music and also helped him to enjoy reading and to fill in the gaps in other aspects of his education.

While at the Royal Academy of Music, Nigel was awarded the Josiah Parker Prize (adjudicated by Sir Michael Tippett) and the Queen's Commendation for Excellence, which is the Royal Academy of Music's highest distinction. Later he was Composition and Contemporary Music tutor at the Academy before becoming Head of Composition at the London College of Music and Media. He has now vacated that position and works full time as a professional composer, work which includes composing film scores. He is also Guest Professor at the Xinjiang Arts Institute in China and is Associate Composer to the Royal Military School of Music, Kneller Hall, amongst many other positions.

Nigel and I had a full day together. We chatted and listened to his music and Nigel explained some of the ways he composes.

As a continuation of the concept of the 'silver lining' of Nigel's journey with dyslexia, he said that there was a sense in which he had been saved by dyslexia; there were so few things he could do that he had to exploit the only areas in which he had any skill and/or success. This had allowed him to be more focused and not to be distracted by things like choices of what he might or might not do. He explained it by saying: 'You have to make the most of what you're good at.' It was a case of trying every chink which might be an opportunity. 'The first thing you have to do is to be honest. You have to be honest with yourself and with others.'

Nigel gave a further reason as to why his dyslexia was now no problem. This was because of the technology available nowadays. He paid further tribute to his teachers named in 'Silver lining', particularly to his hero Paul Patterson and others. He then added the name of the late Peggy Hubicki, for whom he clearly felt much affection and gratitude. He said she had helped him to develop and use his strengths to compensate for his weaknesses.

Nigel explained and demonstrated how he employs the musical-processing system Sibelius for composing, although he does sometimes use longhand methods if it suits or he feels so inclined. He also showed me how he sets up a computer program for himself while composing film scores in order to fulfil all the necessary highly detailed requirements of doing the job of writing for a film. He paid particular tribute to his film-music writing partner Michael Csanyi-Wills, with whom he collaborated and he also mentioned the contribution made by his agent.

We watched extracts of some films on DVD which included the musical score. (We had previously heard some of these extracts without the pictures.)

Nigel said that a composer is able to make his mistakes in private, which is an advantage for a dyslexic. He starts with an idea – any idea – and tries out ways of working with it, maybe using the technology available or his own musical background. He is open and as diverse as possible at this stage and has a broad range of resources. It is his own territory and he said that he is not as vulnerable as, for example, a cellist who is playing in performance where mistakes are glaringly obvious. The composer has the opportunity to play by his own rules and draw others into his space. He has very specific targets even when he is setting out to achieve something different.

A further requirement of professional success as a composer and musical film score writer is business acumen. Although Nigel did not labour this point, he did refer to the mechanics of this part of what he does. As with any enterprise, the wheels cannot move without money. Films are an industry and the musical score writers are part of the whole. There is considerable expense in purchasing the technology which Nigel requires in order to do the job. The whole process of making films is as much a financial enterprise for all concerned as it is a creative one.

In that we spent much of our time on how dyslexia is no problem to Nigel in doing his job as a musical score composer for the film industry, there was not a great deal of it left for listening to his other compositions. However, we did listen to *Black Fire*, which he described as 'the real me!'

Diana's comments

There can be few statements which give so much joy to those working with dyslexics as those which tell of their successes. It is clear that Nigel has realised his potential. By hook or by crook he has managed to handle his particular pattern of dyslexia in such a way that it no longer stands in his way or prevents him from doing what he wants to do; possibly, too, he has taken advantage of his dyslexia in such a way that its positive aspects, including originality and creativity, have been allowed to flourish. It is a record of triumph over adversity, thanks to an extraordinarily positive attitude.

Nigel persistently refused to accept failure. Like many dyslexics, he worked extremely hard, and although there was a sense in which he attributed the silver lining of his dyslexia to good luck, many readers, like myself, were reminded of the mantra that you make your own luck.

For Nigel, the time in the army appears to have been very significant in many ways; in particular, he integrated with his colleagues and fellow musicians and it also gave him a stable financial basis and encouraged his musical gifts.

Listening to his compositions was a great treat for me. I could see how his music students had benefited from his teaching. He invited me in to share some of the techniques which he had created.

I also had the impression that Nigel had made a leap forward since writing to Joshua five years before. He did not need to elaborate in detail on his journey in reaching the various completed compositions; he allowed me to share his music and left the music to speak for itself.

It is a mighty challenge for the dyslexic to accept their dyslexia and Nigel did this, partly because he had no other choice but also because it gave him a handle on things. He had to run with what he could wherever and whenever he could. In my view, he has turned dyslexia on its head and made it work in his favour. This, however, is no easy ride, but it is one in which he has succeeded and which should be of great encouragement to all other dyslexics, whether in the field of music or elsewhere.

The ability to sustain collaborative creative personal relationships is also an attribute of Nigel's own personality as well as those with whom he works, although he dismisses some of this as being a beneficial side effect of having been in the army.

It helped me to a better understanding of the skills and crafts required in his job. However, although I was hugely impressed by these, I felt, and increasingly feel, his musical creative gift of composition is undervalued by his explanation that it is the use of technology which is the reason why dyslexia is no problem for him. I was allowed to be analytical and critical and, above all, I was allowed to enjoy the music and take from it what I could and wished. This was one of Nigel's achievements, which is a great indicator of his humility. That was, and is, the ultimate exposure of himself and his creativity. It is the summit of a creative professional musician to give all he can possibly give at any one time, in whatever field of music the performer expresses him- or herself. I was allowed to enjoy the music.

Amongst brief extracts which we watched and to which we listened, and which he co-wrote with Michael Csanyi-Wills, were *Jinnah*, starring Christopher Lee and James Fox, and Warner Bros' biggest animation film made outside the USA, *The Little Polar Bear*, to mention only two. Nigel's friend Robin Page, who is mentioned above, often conducts the film scores.

I tried to follow a very full musical score of his, *Black Fire*, as we listened to it. It allowed me to confirm for myself that, whatever credit Nigel gives to his ability to do his job simply to modern technology, it is really his gift as a composer which, along with his own personality, is at the root of his achievements. In *Black Fire* he had free rein. I would like to hear it again. It was a remarkable piece of music and just one of Nigel's compositions.

He briefly told me of some of his others. Although he spends time on writing film scores, his creative, musical gift is realised in writing other works also and these have been very widely performed. This is not just the gift of dyslexia; this is the gift of music. Personally, I feel he subsumes his very considerable musical creativity, hard work, persistence and remarkable and meticulous organisational skills and attention to detail into the word 'technology' – and this is without including his engaging interpersonal and social skills. It also does not really take into account his musical educational experiences.

The wonderful thing is that Nigel has not allowed dyslexia to be an impediment in realising that musical gift but has employed it in so doing. Thus, there is not only a silver lining to dyslexia for Nigel; he has found in it a motivational support on which he has capitalised. Nigel says, 'Hard work and technique can overcome most problems.'

Stella, his wife, and Joshua and his younger brother Emile and their life together are all part of why dyslexia is no problem to him. As Joshua has grown and developed, it appears that he may indeed have inherited dyslexia. If this were not the case, it is likely that thinking about dyslexia would have receded from Nigel's mind because it is no problem for him now. However, dyslexia has been brought back into focus and is being honed as he sees some of Joshua's difficulties and tries to understand them with a view to helping him solve them. He can identify with some problems but knows also that every individual dyslexic has their own specific pattern of difficulties. Both Nigel and Stella are also aware of the gift of dyslexia and are very concerned to help Joshua discover his own gift(s) in the most advantageous milieu in which to develop. They want to foster what he is good at; they do not want him to be judged by rigid and inappropriate standards and are thankful that schools are more dyslexia-friendly nowadays.

Conclusion

What, then, can we learn from Nigel's case?

It is a story of triumph over adversity. Many dyslexics may find it hard to achieve fluent reading and spelling, but few are without skills of some kind, and they can be helped to discover what these skills are.

Nigel was successful at working in collaboration with others. This, I think, was because he was modest and unassuming and was able to be sensitive to the feelings of others. To some dyslexics such sensitivity does not come easily, but it can be learnt and is essential for any dyslexic who forms part of a team.

Nigel needed support and guidance from associates in expressing and articulating his ideas, but he did not allow pressures from others to stifle his creativity. Dyslexics should be encouraged to have confidence in themselves.

Nigel was able to make the best use of available technology and this is an area where dyslexic learners in many different contexts can be given useful guidance.

Finally, he was persevering and never willing to take 'no' for an answer. The ability to persevere despite setbacks is, I am sure, a characteristic of the majority of dyslexics who have made a success of their lives.

Reference

Miles, T.R. and Westcombe, J. (eds) (2001) *Music and Dyslexia: Opening New Doors*, Whurr, London.

Science takes us forward

nineteen

Insights from brain imaging

Katie Overy

Introduction

The human brain is a complex and fascinating organ that remains under intense investigation. Historically, debate about the nature of brain function has revolved around questions such as how the brain relates to the mind, how the brain relates to the body and whether or not different regions of the brain are specialised for specific types of processing. Until a few decades ago, the most common way of examining the latter question in particular was to work with patients who had experienced brain damage. In this way, damage to specific regions of the brain was associated with specific impairments in skill (such as severe difficulties with speech or balance).

More recently, extraordinary developments in brain-imaging technology have made it possible to capture the patterns of brain activity while they actually occur. These techniques are all quite different, relying on electrical signals, magnetic signals, changing oxygen levels and/or blood flow. Consequently, the information gathered by each method is also different, usually either providing accurate information about where activation occurs or accurate information about when it occurs. The combined information from these different techniques is rapidly leading to a new body of knowledge regarding the musical brain, and, indeed, the dyslexic brain.

In this chapter, I will summarise some recent research findings in these areas, beginning with a brief description of some of the most commonly used imaging techniques.

Imaging techniques

Electro-encephalography (EEG)

Since neurons communicate with each other via electrical signals, one way to examine brain activity is to measure the nature of the electrical activity occurring at the scalp. This non-invasive technique uses small electrodes placed over the head (usually using a sort of hair net) that are able to detect the electrical signals from synchronised groups of neurons. This direct measure of neuronal activity provides extremely accurate timing information (less than milliseconds), which is particularly useful for detecting the brain's immediate response to expected or unexpected stimuli.

Magneto-encephalography (MEG)

When activated, neurons produce both an electric signal and also a magnetic field that, in a magnetically shielded room, can be measured by superconductive pick-up coils above the head. In a similar way to EEG, the resulting data can provide extremely accurate timing information about neuronal activity. In addition, though, with appropriate data-analysis techniques MEG data can give accurate information about the location of a signal, to within a few millimetres.

Positron Emission Tomography (PET)

Another feature of brain activity is an increase in blood flow to activated regions, accompanied by an increased supply of oxygen. By injecting a radioactive oxygen compound into the bloodstream, increased blood flow in specific brain regions can be traced with a spatial accuracy of about five millimetres, thus identifying which parts of the brain are involved during certain types of task. One weakness of this method is the temporal resolution, since the timing of the activation cannot be identified with more accuracy than about two minutes. Another considerable drawback is the involvement of a radioactive injection, of which only a limited number can be safely administered during one lifetime.

Functional Magnetic Resonance Imaging (fMRI)

Increased blood flow to a region of activated neurons results in a decrease in the proportion of *de*oxygenated haemoglobin in that region. Since oxygenated and deoxygenated haemoglobin have different magnetic properties, this change can be detected (in the presence of a large magnetic field, the MRI brain scanner) and used to provide extremely accurate spatial information (between one and three millimetres) about which parts of the brain are activated during specific cognitive tasks. This makes fMRI a very powerful form of brain imaging, although the reliance on blood flow means that the temporal resolution of the technique is not very fast (about three to eight seconds).

Neural processing of music

With the development of the brain-imaging techniques described above, there has been a surge of scientific interest in the musical brain. While research is still very much in progress, there is a growing consensus that musical experience activates many different regions of the brain, since it involves highly complex perceptual, cognitive and motor skills, in addition to aesthetic and emotional responses. In order to examine such processes experimentally, it is usually necessary to isolate one element of musical experience at a time, requiring the design of very specific musical tasks (such as identifying whether or not two short melodies are the same, or identifying when a 'wrong' musical chord is heard) and examining how the brain behaves during their execution. This kind of experiment has led to a wide variety of research findings, which increase in their detail and diversity as brain-imaging techniques and new experimental designs continue to develop.

Perhaps one of the most explored areas of musical processing to date is melody perception. For example, a number of fMRI and PET studies have found that melody tasks seem to engage the right auditory cortex more predominantly than the left auditory cortex (see Zatorre, 2003). Although this right-hemisphere lateralisation for melody is not found consistently across all studies, it perhaps explains why music has traditionally been associated with the right hemisphere of the brain (based on early evidence from brain-damaged patients, for example). Harmonic processing has also been found to show a right-hemisphere dominance, for example various EEG studies have found more prominent activation in the right frontal regions of the brain during the detection of incongruous chords in a harmonic sequence (for example Koelsch *et al.*, 2000). However, some fMRI studies of pitch memory have found regions in the left side of the brain to be more predominantly activated (for example Gaab *et al.*, 2003). This exemplifies the complex nature of musical processing, which is distributed across many regions of the brain, including both the left and right cerebral hemispheres. It also exemplifies the fact that music can show different neural activation patterns depending on the specific design of the experimental musical task.

Rhythm processing has not yet received the same research attention as melody processing, but interest in this area is growing. One particularly interesting finding is the discovery that rhythmic listening tasks seem to activate motor regions of the brain in addition to auditory regions. For example, fMRI studies examining the difference between regular and irregular rhythms have found that rhythms with a strong regular beat show more activation of the basal ganglia, an area of the brain known to be involved in generating movement (Grahn and Brett, 2007). Other tasks, such as comparing rhythms or tapping to rhythms, have been found to activate the cerebellum, a region traditionally associated with balance, timing and motor control, as well as the pre-motor cortex, which is involved in preparing for movement (Parsons, 2001; Sakai *et al.*, 1999). Another interesting finding is that certain temporal aspects of music appear to show some lateralisation towards left-hemisphere brain regions, which have traditionally been associated with language skills. Together with a body of related research, this has led Zatorre and Belin (2001) to hypothesise that the left auditory cortex is specialised for rapid temporal information in both speech and music, while the right auditory cortex is specialised for spectral or pitch information in both speech and music, thus challenging the traditional view that language is wholly left lateralised and music is wholly right lateralised.

In fact, there is increasing evidence that music and language share certain neural resources, which is perhaps not surprising when one considers their similar characteristics. Both are forms of auditory human communication in which single perceptual units are combined according to complex cultural rules and hierarchies to create meaningful sequences. Thus, both rely on a similar range of perceptual and cognitive skills, including short-term auditory memory and long-term auditory learning. One brain region of particular interest here is a left-hemisphere frontal region known as Broca's area, which is well established as a language region of the brain centrally involved in speech production. An increasing number of neuro-imaging studies have found Broca's area to be activated during musical listening tasks, such as rhythm processing and melodic and harmonic discrimination (Platel *et al.*, 1997; Brown and Martinez, 2006). It has also been found that musicians show increased activation in this network (Bangert *et al.*, 2006), which lends some support to the numerous studies suggesting that musicians tend to outperform non-musicians on language tasks (Chan *et al.*, 1998; Kilgour *et al.*, 2000) and also leads to fascinating questions about the potential effects of musical training on the brain.

Neural differences associated with musical training

One major reason for an increasing amount of research into the musical brain is the current scientific interest in neural plasticity, that is the potential of the brain to change in response to its environment. Musicians are a particularly interesting experimental group for this type of work, since they spend thousands of hours practising over many years, developing not only expert musicianship but also extraordinary motor skills. A number of studies comparing the brain structure of musicians and non-musicians have found certain differences, with musicians exhibiting signs of increased left lateralisation of the left planum temporale (part of the auditory cortex), increased volume in a region of the cerebellum (involved in timing and motor control) and increased volume in the front part of the corpus callosum (which connects and transfers information between the two hemispheres) (see Schlaug, 2001). Further studies have suggested that musicians show increased grey matter (indicating the amount of neurons present) in Broca's area and in the primary auditory cortex (Sluming *et al.*, 2002; Schneider *et al.*, 2002). Although it has not been demonstrated that such structural brain differences are actually caused by musical training (on the contrary, they may simply facilitate excellent musical performance), there is increasing evidence to suggest that training may be a key factor. For example, it has been shown that the regions of the motor cortex responsible for hand movements are more prominent in the left-hand region for violinists and in the right-hand region for pianists, suggesting that the type of instrument played (and the associated repetitive motor movements) may affect the type of brain differences observed (Bangert and Schlaug, 2006).

In a similar way, musicians and non-musicians are often found to show different neural activation patterns during musical processing. For example, musicians have been found to show stronger left-hemisphere lateralisation during general musical-listening tasks, as well as during specific rhythm perception tasks (Evers *et al.*, 1999; Vusst *et al.*, 2005). EEG and MEG studies have also demonstrated that musicians tend to exhibit faster and stronger neural responses to musical stimuli, such as melodic changes and harmonically inappropriate chords (Pantev *et al.*, 2003; Koelsch *et al.*, 2002). It is possible, of course, that such activation differences are an indicator of innate musical ability, but it is increasingly suggested that such differences are more likely to be due to the effects of training and increased exposure to music. Many studies find greater differences with the early onset of training and an increased number of years of practice, while one recent study has shown that just one year of violin lessons can lead to faster and stronger neural responses to violin tones in young children (Fujioka *et al.*, 2006).

Perhaps most interesting of all is the fact that musicians can also show differences in neural activation patterns during non-musical tasks. Broca's area, for example (involved in speech production, as discussed above), seems to show stronger activation in musicians compared to non-musicians during spatio-temporal reasoning tasks and rapid temporal processing tasks (Sluming *et al.*, 2007; Gaab *et al.*, 2005), while even the brain stem of musicians has been found to respond more effectively to speech signals (Wong *et al.*, 2007). Recent work has also shown that children with musical training show stronger neural responses to language stimuli (Jentschke *et al.*, 2005), while a discussion in the journal *Trends in Neurosciences* (Tallal and Gaab, 2006) outlines a range of evidence in support of the proposal that musical training improves auditory processing and language development (Overy, 2003). Such developments have significant implications for the potential use of music as a language-support tool for dyslexia, as discussed in Chapter 4.

Neural differences associated with dyslexia

The neural differences underlying developmental dyslexia have been discussed for many years, with some controversy. Since the specific nature of dyslexia-related deficits (and strengths) remain under discussion, with definitions and diagnostic criteria still being updated, it is not a simple matter to compare a group of dyslexic adults with non-dyslexic adults and identify the key neural differences. In addition, the variability of language and literacy abilities in any group of dyslexic individuals has been found to have a significant effect on any neural differences identified. However, despite these difficulties, much research has been conducted in this area and both structural differences and functional activation differences are commonly found to be associated with dyslexia.

For example, the cerebellum is often implicated in dyslexia, with various studies reporting certain regions to be slightly smaller, to have less grey matter and to show weaker activation during language tasks. Broca's area has also been found to show less grey matter and to have a smaller surface area and weaker activation during language tasks. The inferior parietal area (which is located just above the planum temporale and is involved in multisensory integration) has also been found to show differences, with some data suggesting that it can be larger or more left-lateralised, particularly in high-achieving dyslexic adults. Other reports have suggested that the planum temporale may be less strongly lateralised to the left hemisphere and that the corpus callosum may be slightly smaller in certain areas, although there is conflicting evidence regarding these brain regions in particular (see Eckert, 2004 for a review of this anatomical research).

Despite the complexity of such findings, it is clear from the scientific literature that there is a general trend for dyslexic adults and children to show slightly weaker and delayed neural responses to language and language-related auditory stimuli (for example Kujala *et al.*, 2000; Bonte *et al.*, 2006), while showing less left-lateralised activation for language (for example Cao *et al.*, 2006). Indeed, many studies have found evidence of right-lateralisation for language tasks (for example Spironelli *et al.*, 2006; Dufor *et al.*, 2007), lending some support to claims that dyslexia is associated with right-hemisphere strengths such as global visuo-spatial ability (von Karolyi *et al.*, 2003). The various positive abilities reported to be associated with dyslexia are only just beginning to be identified experimentally, and so the neural basis of such strengths presents a promising new area for future research.

Another important area of current research is the examination of the neural effects of language-training programmes. A few recent studies have found that, after specific phonological or auditory training, dyslexic children and adults show increased activity in left-hemisphere language regions (Eden *et al.*, 2004) and stronger and faster neural responses to language-related auditory stimuli (Kujala *et al.*, 2001). Such findings demonstrate the incredible plasticity of the human brain, which is capable of learning and adapting throughout the lifespan in response to experience and training. This in turn lends powerful support to suggestions that musical training might affect the neural basis of language processing.

Discussion

It is apparent from the research presented in this chapter that investigations into the mechanisms of the human brain are not a simple matter. Indeed, for many of the studies mentioned, it would be possible to find a similar study reporting a contradictory finding. It is also apparent that musical performance involves many different regions of the brain, which may explain why dyslexic musicians can exhibit extraordinary strengths in some areas of musicality while experiencing difficulties in other areas. For example, reports that timing skills can be problematic in dyslexia may be partly linked to the role of the cerebellum in musical timing, since the cerebellum has been identified as a region of the brain implicated in dyslexia. The cerebellum is also responsible for gross-motor movement, which might help to explain why dyslexic children seem to benefit from learning to 'feel' rhythms using large body movements (Oglethorpe, 1996). Dyslexic musicians' reported difficulties with sight-reading may also be partly explained: the discovery of the numerous regions of the brain involved in sight-reading at the piano has led to the suggestion that this may be one of the most complex multisensory activities conducted by humans (Sergent *et al.*, 1992)!

It should be noted, though, that two important components of musical experience have not been discussed here: the emotional and social aspects of music, which can be profound and, indeed, are often the primary motivations for either performing or listening to music. Research into the neural basis of emotional responses to music suggests that the core emotional systems of the brain are involved (Blood and Zatorre, 2001), while the neural mechanisms of social music-making remain at the speculative level but may involve regions of the brain known as the mirror neuron system, which itself engages with perceptual and emotional regions (Molnar-Szakacs and Overy, 2006). There is no doubt that future research into these elements of musical experience will provide further valuable insights into the nature of the musical, dyslexic brain.

References

Bangert, M. and Schlaug, G. (2006) Specialization of the specialized in features of external brain morphology. *European Journal of Neuroscience* **24**(6): 1832–1834.

Bangert, M., Peschel, T., Schlaug, G., Rotte, M. *et al.* (2006) Shared networks for auditory and motor processing in professional pianists: evidence from fMRI conjunction. *Neuroimage* **30**(3): 917–926.

Blood, A.J. and Zatorre, R.J. (2001) Intensely pleasurable responses to music correlate with activity in brain regions implicated with reward and emotion. *Proceedings of the National Academy of Sciences* **98**(20): 11818–11823.

Bonte, M., Parviainen, T., Hytönen, K. and Salmelin, R. (2006) Time course of top-down and bottom-up influences on syllable processing in the auditory cortex. *Cerebral Cortex* **16**(1): 115–123.

Brown, S. and Martinez, M. (2006) Activation of premotor vocal areas during musical discrimination. *Brain and Cognition* **63**(1): 59–69.

Cao, F., Bitan, T., Chou, T.L., Burman, D.D. and Booth, J.R. (2006) Deficient orthographic and phonological representations in children with dyslexia revealed by brain activation patterns. *Journal of Child Psychology and Psychiatry* **47**(10): 1041–1050.

Chan, A.S., Ho,Y-C. and Cheung, M-C. (1998) Music training improves verbal memory. *Nature* **396**(November): 128.

Dufor, O. (2007) Top-down processes during auditory phoneme categorization in dyslexia: a PET study. *Neuroimage* **34**(4): 1692–16707.

Eckert, M. (2004) Neuroanatomical markers for dyslexia: a review of dyslexia structural imaging studies. *The Neuroscientist* **10**(4): 362–371.

Eden, G.F., Jones, K.M., Cappell, K., Gareau, L. *et al.* (2004) Neural changes following remediation in adult developmental dyslexia. *Neuron* **44**(3): 411–422.

Evers, S., Dannert, J., Rödding, D., Rötter, G. and Ringelstein, E.B. (1999) The cerebral haemodynamics of music perception: a transcranial Doppler sonography study. *Brain: A Journal of Neurology* **122**(Part 1): 75–85.

Fujioka, T., Ross, B., Kakigi, R., Pantev, C. and Trainor, L.J. (2006) One year of musical training affects development of auditory cortical-evoked fields in young children. *Brain: A Journal of Neurology* **129**(10): 2593–2608.

Gaab, N., Gaser, C., Zaehle, T., Jaenke, L. and Schlaug, G. (2003) Functional anatomy of pitch memory: an fMRI study with sparse temporal sampling. *Neuroimage* **19**(4): 1417–1426.

Gaab, N., Tallal, P., Kim, H., Lakshminarayanan, K. *et al.* (2005) Neural correlates of rapid spectrotemporal processing in musicians and nonmusicians. *Annals of the New York Academy of Sciences* **1060**(December): 82–88.

Grahn, J.A. and Brett, M. (2007) Rhythm and beat perception in motor areas of the brain. *Journal of Cognitive Neuroscience* **19**(5): 893–906.

Jentschke, S., Koelsch, S. and Friederici, A.D. (2005) Neural correlates of processing structure in music and language: influences of musical training and language impairment. *Annals of the New York Academy of Sciences*, **1060**(December): 231–242.

Kilgour, A.R., Jakobson, L.S. and Cuddy, L.L. (2000) Music training and rate of presentation as mediators of text and song recall. *Memory & Cognition* **28**(5): 700–710.

Koelsch, S., Gunter, T., Friederici, A.D. and Schroger, E. (2000) Brain indices of music processing: 'nonmusicians' are musical. *Journal of Cognitive Neuroscience* **12**(3): 520–541.

Koelsch, S., Schmidt, B.H. and Kansok, J. (2002) Effect of musical expertise on the early right anterior negativity: an event related brain potential study. *Psychophysiology* **27**(2): 308–314.

Kujala, T., Karma, K., Ceponiene, R., Belitz, S. *et al.* (2001) Plastic neural changes and reading improvement caused by audio-visual training in reading-impaired children. *Proceedings of the National Academy of Sciences* **98**(18): 10509–10514.

Kujala, T., Myllyviita, K., Tervaniemi, M., Alho, K. *et al.* (2000) Basic auditory dysfunction in dyslexia as demonstrated by brain activity measurements. *Psychophysiology* **37**(2): 262–266.

Molnar-Szakacs, I. and Overy, K. (2006) Music and mirror neurons: from motion to 'e'motion. *Social Cognitive and Affective Neuroscience* **1**(3): 235–241.

Oglethorpe, S. (1996) *Instrumental Music for Dyslexics: A Teaching Handbook*, Whurr, London.

Overy, K. (2003) Dyslexia and music: from timing deficits to musical intervention. *Annals of the New York Academy of Sciences* **999**(November): 497–505.

Pantev, C., Ross, B., Fujiko, T., Trainor, L.J. *et al.* (2003) Musical and learning-induced cortical plasticity. *Annals of the New York Academy of Sciences* **999**(November): 438–450.

Parsons, L.M. (2001) Exploring the functional neuroanatomy of music performance, perception, and comprehension. *Annals of the New York Academy of Sciences* **930**(June): 11–31.

Platel, H., Price, C., Baron, J-C., Wise, R. *et al.* (1997) The structural components of music perception: a functional anatomical study. *Brain: A Journal of Neurology* **120**(Part 2): 229–243.

Sakai, K., Hikosaka, O., Miyauchi, S., Takino, R. *et al.* (1999) Neural representation of a rhythm depends on its interval ratio. *Journal of Neuroscience* **19**(22): 10074–10081.

Schlaug, G. (2001) The brain of musicians: a model for functional and structural adaptation. *Annals of the New York Academy of Sciences* **930**(June): 281–299.

Schneider, P., Scherg, M., Dosch, H.G., Specht, H.J. *et al.* (2002) Morphology of Heschl's gyrus reflects enhanced activation in the auditory cortex of musicians. *Nature Neuroscience* **5**(7): 688–694.

Sergent, J., Zuck, E., Terriah, S. and McDonald, B. (1992) Distributed neural network underlying musical sight-reading and keyboard performance. *Science* **257**(5066): 106–109.

Sluming, V., Barrick, T., Howard, M., Cezayirli, E. *et al.* (2002) Voxel-based morphometry reveals increased gray matter density in Broca's area in male symphony orchestra musicians. *Neuroimage* **17**(3): 1613–1622.

Sluming, V., Brooks, J., Howard, M., Downes, J.J. and Robert, N. (2007) Broca's area supports enhanced visuospatial cognition in orchestral musicians. *Journal of Neuroscience* **27**(14): 3799–3806.

Spironelli, C., Renolazzi, B., Voi, C. and Angrilli, A. (2006) Inverted EEG lateralisation in dyslexic children during phonological processing. *Neuropsychologia* **44**(14): 2812–2821.

Tallal, P. and Gaab, N. (2006) Dynamic auditory processing, musical experience and language development. *Trends in Neurosciences* **29**(7): 382–390.

Von Karolyi, C., Winner, E., Gray, W. and Sherman, G.F. (2003) Dyslexia linked to talent: global visual-spatial ability. *Brain and Language* **85**(3): 427–431.

Vuust, P., Pallesen, K.J., Bailey, C., van Zuijen, T. *et al.* (2005) To musicians, the message is in the meter. *Neuroimage* **24**(2): 560–564.

Wong, P.C.M., Skoe, E., Russo, N.M., Dees, T. and Kraus, N. (2007) Musical experience shapes human brainstem encoding of linguistic pitch patterns. *Nature Neuroscience* **10**(4): 420–422.

Zatorre, R.J. (2003) Neural specializations for tonal processing. In: *The Cognitive Neuroscience of Music*, I. Peretz and R. Zatorre (eds), Oxford University Press, Oxford.

Zatorre, R.J. and Belin, P. (2001) Spectral and temporal processing in the human auditory cortex. *Cerebral Cortex* **11**(10): 946–953.

twenty

Music reading: a cognitive neuroscience approach

Lauren Stewart

The fact that many dyslexic children and adults are engaged in music, and often go on to reach high levels of success, illustrates that dyslexia need not be a barrier to achieving high levels of musical accomplishment. However, despite this, there is growing anecdotal evidence from teachers, parents and students (Miles and Westcombe, 2001) that many dyslexic musicians have particular difficulties with the notational aspects of musical learning. In the same way that theories of dyslexia (for example the phonological deficit hypothesis) emerged on the basis of psychological models of the normal reading process, it is critical to have an understanding of how normal music reading occurs. Once we know the building blocks involved in skilled music reading, it will be possible to test the competency of each of these aspects in those with dyslexia to determine which aspects cause the most trouble to dyslexic music students, and where alternative teaching strategies are needed. With this in mind, the following chapter is concerned with reviewing what we know about the psychological and neurological aspects of music reading.

Musical scores are, as a rule, read in order to perform them. However, the outcome of a musical performance depends on many factors besides an accurate reading of the score. General musical ability and the number of hours spent practising the piece are just two additional factors. How then is it possible to look at music reading in isolation from these other factors which influence musical performance? One way to do this would be to present the musician with a written score and ask them to play the piece with little or no preparation. Musicians, even of equivalent instrumental proficiency, will perform this task with varying degrees of success. The fact that accurate sight-reading performance cannot be accounted for purely by instrumental proficiency tells us that the psychological processes involved in music reading and music playing are distinct.

In order to get an idea of how music reading is achieved, one approach has been to ask what it is that skilled sight-readers do differently from weaker sight-readers at the same level of musical proficiency. Measurement of the eye–hand span in pianists provides a measure of the difference, in terms of notes played or time elapsed between the position of the eyes and the position of the hands in the musical score, at a given point in time. To demonstrate that the eyes are normally ahead of the hands during music reading, simply remove the musical score while a musician is sight-reading. Invariably, performance continues for several seconds, implying that the brain has prepared and stored the relevant instructions for performance of several notes in advance of the point at which the music is removed. The number of extra notes which can be played after the music is removed appears to relate to sight-reading skill. Pianists who perform sight-reading more accurately can play more notes after removal of the score compared to pianists who are less skilled at sight-reading. They have a larger eye–hand span (Sloboda, 1974).

So, those musicians who look further ahead in the music do better at sight-reading. However, it would be a mistake to think that some musicians are better sight-readers simply because they look further ahead in the score. A wealth of experiments concerning eye movements in text reading tells us that the pattern of eye movements made does not determine the rate at which our brain can process the information that it receives, rather that the pattern of eye movements *reflects* the rate at which the brain processes this information. A finding which illustrates this is that the eye–hand span can vary in the same individual depending on the complexity and/or familiarity of the piece, constricting with simple, familiar and tonal music and expanding with complex, unfamiliar and atonal music.

In order to discover the potential source of individual differences in sight-reading, it is necessary to first consider what kind of task sight-reading can be considered to be. In his treatise, 'On reading music', Lowery (1940) likens it to an exercise in pattern recognition:

We are led to the idea of pattern reading in which groups of notes are recognised as being melodically and harmonically related so that the occurrence of two or more notes of the group forming the pattern may be taken as symbolic of the whole and their recognition renders further reading of the constituent notes unnecessary.

This view is echoed, anecdotally, by practising musicians and has some experimental support. For instance, when musicians and non-musicians are presented with notated musical excerpts for a short time and required to copy them, musicians are significantly better than non-musicians at remembering information about the shape of the note sequences than non-musicians, suggesting that this is how they read music when they have to perform it (Sloboda, 1978). Sight-reading may therefore involve grouping notes together to form a 'chunk'. All the notes within a chunk can be processed at the same time but separate chunks must be dealt with consecutively. For this reason, it is more efficient, in terms of brain processing, to parse the musical score into larger, fewer chunks. A model of sight-reading (Wolf, 1976) suggests that knowledge acquired over years of practice with different musical structures becomes stored in memory and can be brought to bear on sight-reading performance. As the eyes scan the musical score, an attempt is made to match musical structures present in the notation with knowledge in memory concerning how to play such structures. For example, an arpeggio starting on D may be spotted easily, because of its distinctive visual pattern. Once detected, the reader can call up the instructions for playing this structure from memory, leaving the eyes to scan further ahead, looking for yet more chunks in the music.

This pattern-matching process is strongly affected by the reader's musical knowledge concerning, for instance, the musical style and/or structure of the piece. Lowery (1940) writes:

[I]f the reader has some perception of the composer's intentions, he will expect to hear certain groupings of notes which constitute part of musical sentences.

Evidence of this comes from the demonstration of 'proofreader's error' in music reading, a phenomenon first noted by the distinguished pianist Boris Goldovsky. While giving a music lesson, Goldovsky was irritated by a pupil who repeatedly and consistently played the wrong note at a certain place in Brahms' *Capriccio*. After several futile attempts to correct this assumed deviation from the score, Goldovsky realised that the pupil had in fact produced an accurate rendition, since the score contained a misprint (a G rather than a G#) at this particular point. Struck by the fact that the misprint had gone unnoticed by all his previous pupils, Goldovsky challenged a group of professional pianists to find the misprint, allowing them to play the piece as many times as they liked. Unlike Goldovsky's pupil, the professional pianists all played the music as it should have been written, not as it was actually written. Rather than playing the notes one by one, they segmented the score into chunks, guided by their knowledge concerning the kinds of musical structures that could be expected in a piece of Brahms piano music. The process of chunking and the influence of musical knowledge on this process resulted in the misprint being overlooked. It is telling that the musical novice, who was probably chunking the music less effectively compared to the professional pianists, was able to produce an accurate, though less musical, rendition.

If sight-reading involves the matching of musical patterns (or chunks) in the score to instructions for the performance of these patterns in memory, differences in sight-reading ability may result for several reasons. By analogy, one can imagine that musicians possess a dictionary of visual musical patterns and a dictionary of corresponding instructions for the performance of those patterns. Stronger sight-readers may possess a larger number of entries for either or both dictionaries. Alternatively, the number of entries may be equivalent between good and poor sight-readers, but the speed at which the corresponding visual and motor entries are matched may differ. A third possibility may be that the better sight-readers may possess a greater knowledge of musical style and structure, or may use such knowledge more effectively, in order to form expectations regarding which musical patterns are likely or unlikely to occur – the equivalent to only searching within a single section of the dictionary corresponding to the relevant musical style, rather than searching all entries for all possible musical styles.

In addition to asking 'What makes a good sight-reader?', it is also important to ask, 'What makes any kind of music reader, let alone a good one?' How do our brains deal with the task of decoding a set of visual symbols (musical notes), ascribing some meaning to them and then mapping them onto the appropriate set of musical responses?

Some of my own work has been able to address this question. A few years ago, I recruited a group of 15 musically untrained adults. Using standardised teaching and assessment methods, I taught them to read music and play keyboard to Grade 1 standard. Before and after learning, I would compare how their brains responded to seeing musical notation, in order to investigate how the process of acquiring musical literacy changes brain function.

The kind of brain imaging I intended to use, functional magnetic resonance imaging (fMRI), is based on the concept that different parts of the brain are designed to deal with different types of information. While there is no simple one-to-one relationship between brain regions and different aspects of human behaviour (as the phrenologists advocated in the eighteenth century), there is, however, some division of labour. The pattern of activity seen in the brain depends upon the type of task in which the brain is engaged. A typical fMRI study involves the measurement of brain activity while a volunteer performs a task of interest inside the scanner, for example a language task, an arithmetic task or a visual task. My study would measure brain activity as volunteers were engaged in music-reading tasks. By having the volunteers perform the same tasks before and after musical training, I aimed to determine training-related changes in the brain's response to musical notation. To ensure that any difference in brain activity between the two scanning sessions could not be attributed to general effects of scanning people twice (for instance people may be more relaxed the second time round), I also scanned a control group of volunteers who could not read or play music and were not included in the training part of the study.

I chose to engage the learners in three different types of music-reading task, before and after training. Task one required learners to decode notated melodies that were devoid of rhythm (all notes were crotchets), while task two required learners to decode notated rhythms which were devoid of melody (each rhythm was notated on the same pitch). Both these tasks required music reading and performance on a small keyboard, which was specially adapted for use in the high magnetic field environment of the fMRI scanner. In contrast, task three required neither music reading nor performance. Instead, learners detected a particular visual feature amidst musical notation. This non-musical task allowed me to ask whether brain changes would be seen after musical training even when the musical notation was merely incidental to the task.

The volunteer learners attended a music lesson every week for three months, completed theory exercises for homework and practised for at least half an hour, three times a week. Although this was asking a lot of them – many had full-time teaching and lecturing jobs – a change in the brain's activity in response to musical notation depended upon each and every one of them learning to successfully decode musical notation. The second set of brain scans was already booked for three months ahead – it was literally a race against time to change their brains.

Progress varied from one learner to the next, as did the pattern of strengths and weaknesses across the group. Nevertheless, all 12 learners reached the required standard of Grade 1 theory and keyboard (Associated Board of the Royal Schools of Music), as assessed by an external music teacher. This was convincing evidence that learning had occurred. Even so, the Associated Board Grade examination is a global measure of musical skill, requiring candidates to perform prepared pieces of music, execute specified scales and arpeggios and sight-read. As a psychological measure, which would specifically relate to music reading,

I devised the musical Stroop task (Stewart *et al.*, 2004), based on a similar Stroop task that has been used in language research since the 1930s (Stroop, 1935).

In the musical Stroop task, each learner sat in front of a keyboard, with the fingers of the right hand over the notes G, A, B, C and D. A musical bar containing a random assortment of the notes G, A, B, C, D appeared on a computer screen. On each note, a number, either 1, 2, 3, 4 or 5, was superimposed. The learners were asked to ignore the musical notes and to pay attention to the numbers alone, using them to make a sequence of keypresses. They were told to associate the number 1 with a keypress made by the thumb, the number 2 with a keypress made by the index finger and so on. Once all five keypresses had been made, another bar of notes would appear and the learners would continue in the same way. The crucial feature of the experiment was that sometimes the numbers and notes would coincide and sometimes they would not. In cases where the numbers and notes coincided, the number 1 would be superimposed on the note G, the number 2 would be superimposed on the note A, and so on, so that both the notes and the numbers would specify the same sequence of keypresses. In cases where the numbers and notes did not coincide, the number 4 might be superimposed on the note G, the number 1 might be superimposed on the note A, and so on, so that the notes and numbers specified a different sequence of keypresses.

Even though the learners were instructed to ignore the musical notes in all conditions, the prediction was that when the notes and numbers coincided, specifying the same sequence of keypresses, the learners would be quicker to execute the sequence of keypresses compared to when the notes and numbers specified a different sequence of keypresses. This prediction was based on evidence from the classic Stroop task that literate individuals cannot ignore the written word. If the word 'red' is written in blue ink and people are asked to name the ink colour, they are slower to say 'blue' compared with the situation in which the string of letters 'XXX' is written in blue ink. Despite instructions to disregard the word itself and focus only on its colour, the brain automatically processes the written word and the tendency to say the word 'red' must be suppressed. Musical literacy might, I thought, have a similar effect in the analogous musical Stroop task. Once musical notes have acquired some meaning, their presence would be impossible to ignore, with consequent effects on the speed at which a sequence of keypresses could be made.

A comparison of the speed at which the learners made a sequence of keypresses in the two contrasting situations – when the notes and numbers coincided and when they did not – showed that they were considerably faster in the former case, relative to the latter. In contrast, the speed at which non-musicians made a sequence of keypresses did not differ according to whether the notes and numbers coincided. Non-musicians were oblivious to whether the notes and the numbers specified the same sequence of keypresses because, for them, musical notes did not specify any sequence of keypresses at all.

Taking this experiment a step further, the two groups were also compared on a similar Stroop task in which number-to-finger mapping was pitted against a spatial stimulus-to-response mapping (Stewart *et al.*, 2004). Numbers, again between 1 and 5, appeared in vertical positions that were either congruent or incongruent with respect to the required response. For instance, a '5' appearing in the uppermost vertical position (and requiring a keypress with the little finger) would be congruent for pianists, since notes appearing higher up the stave are mapped to more rightward responses on the keyboard. A '5' appearing in the lowermost vertical position (also requiring a keypress with the little finger) would be incongruent, since notes appearing lower down the stave are mapped to more leftward responses.

Pianists, but not non-musicians, showed a response-time difference between the congruent and incongruent conditions. In other words, they showed evidence of having developed a set of vertical-to-horizontal stimulus-to-response mappings. It seems that the demands of constantly mapping from musical notes (the pitch of which is organised in vertical space) to a set of response elements (keys of the piano) which vary in horizontal space forges a set of spatial mappings which are in evidence even outside a musical context.

Both the Grade 1 examination results and the musical Stroop task showed that the training had achieved its aim of instilling knowledge of music notation. But how was this reflected in terms of changes in brain activity? To answer this I scanned the learners and non-learners for a second time, and, for each group, compared the data from each of the three tasks before and after training. The results of this comparison showed that the brain of the now music-literate learners had changed in a very specific way (Stewart *et al.*, 2003). Some of the changes were specific to the task, while some changes were seen in more than one task.

In task one, where learners decoded musical melodies, a small area in the superior parietal lobe of the brain became active after learning, while it remained inactive in people who had not been taught. This area specialises in dealing with spatial information, especially when the spatial co-ordinates must be used to organise our behaviour. For instance, catching a ball requires the brain to convert information about the spatial location of the ball and its trajectory into instructions for the movement system. While I would not claim that reading music for melody is akin to catching a ball, both may be argued to belong to the same broad category of behaviours. Reading music for melody, like catching a ball, requires spatial information (the position of a note on the stave) to be converted into a movement (selection of the appropriate keypress). The brain specialisations that allow us to move around in space and react to events occurring in our environment are found in other animals and are present from birth in humans. Music reading, as a culturally acquired activity, seems to have taken advantage of this pre-existing specialisation for the use of spatial information to organise musical responses.

In task two, where learners decoded musical rhythms, an area in the occipital region of the brain was active after training. This area is known to be important for making visual discriminations. For instance, in order to distinguish different species of bird, we have to rely on relatively small differences in their visual appearance. In the same way, reading musical rhythms relies upon distinguishing between small visual features: how many tails are present on the note stem? Is there a dot after the note? When reading notation for melody, spatial information is important; when reading notation for rhythm, visual features are important. Of course, music is normally read for both melody and rhythm simultaneously, and future studies will be able to determine how the brain combines both spatial and visual feature information to produce a single musical response that is integrated in space and time.

Tasks one and two required the learners to read and play from musical notation. Task three required neither. Instead, it was a visual task embedded within musical notation. Would training cause changes in the brain's response to musical notation, even when the notation is incidental to the task? The answer was 'yes' – two areas of the brain were active after training, specifically in the learners'. One of these areas, the superior parietal cortex, was identical to the area activated in task one. The other area was in a different area of the parietal lobe, called the supramarginal gyrus, which is known to have a role in the preparatory stages of movement. In the context of task three, these two different brain activations imply that simply seeing musical notes after training sets in motion a whole string of neural events related to the learnt musical responses conveyed by the musical notation. Just like the results of the musical Stroop experiment, these changes in brain activity show that musical training causes notes to acquire a significance that cannot be suppressed.

The above consideration of music reading suggests some candidate areas of difficulty for the dyslexic musical learner. In particular, music reading requires fast, automatic translation between spatial (pitch) and featural (rhythm) information on the stave, and a set of instrument-specific responses. Skilled music readers achieve a degree of fluency that allow them to produce the appropriate musical response to one chunk while they are already looking ahead and preparing the musical response to the next. They use top-down knowledge to avoid having to translate every note, instead preparing the appropriate response on the basis of a pattern they have detected (for example an arpeggio or scale), giving them a shortcut. Each of these is a potential problem area for dyslexics, who, as with word reading, may have to rely on slower, more explicit strategies to achieve the same musical performance. Although there is more work still to do in order to fully characterise all the cognitive processes that are involved in music reading (for instance how information from the spatial and featural aspects of notation are combined), there is some foundation on which to build on the valuable anecdotal reports from dyslexic musicians to formally investigate which aspects of music reading present the most difficulty for dyslexic learners. Once this challenge has been met, the stage will be set for an evidence-based development of alternative teaching strategies for dyslexic musicians.

References

Lowery, H. (1940) On reading music. *Dioptric Review and British Journal of Physiological Optic* **1**: 78–88.

Miles, T.R. and Westcombe, J. (2001) (eds) *Music and Dyslexia: Opening New Doors*, Whurr, London.

Sloboda, J.A. (1978) Perception of contour in music reading. *Perception* **7**(3): 323–331.

Sloboda, J.A. (1974) The eye–hand span: an approach to the study of sight-reading. *Psychology of Music* **2**: 4–10.

Stewart, L., Henson, R., Kampe, K., Walsh, V. *et al.* (2003) Becoming a pianist: brain changes associated with learning to read and play music. *Neuroimage* **20**: 71–83.

Stewart, L., Walsh, V. and Frith, U. (2004) Reading music modifies spatial mapping in pianists. *Perception and Psychophysics* **66**(2): 183–195.

Stroop, J.R. (1935) Studies of interference in serial verbal reactions. *Journal of Experimental Psychology* **18**: 662.

Wolf, T. (1976) A cognitive model of musical sight-reading. *Journal of Psycholinguistic Research* **5**(2): 143–171.

Index

(Note: Individual instruments are listed under the entry 'Instruments'.)

LE LIVRE DE C[ ]
DU RÉGIME PALÉO

50 recettes savoureuses faciles à
préparer réduisent l'inflammation, se
sentent plus jeunes et brûlent les
graisses plus rapidement avec les
aliments de nos ancêtres

FABRICE THOMAS

TABLE DES MATIÈRES

INTRODUCTION

Le régime paléo est un régime qui élimine les allergènes alimentaires courants de l'alimentation. Il s'agit principalement de blé et de lactose de lait contenant du gluten et de caséine. De plus, les légumineuses sont interdites - elles sont également capables de perturber les intestins.

Le régime paléo signifie éviter les céréales, le pain, les produits de boulangerie, les produits laitiers - et même les arachides et le soja (ils appartiennent aux légumineuses). Alors, quels sont les avantages du régime paléo pour le corps - et quels aliments êtes-vous autorisé à manger ?

Le régime paléo consiste à abandonner les aliments « modernes » et à passer aux aliments traditionnels. Le nom "paléo" fait référence à la période paléolithique, qui a duré 2,5 millions d'années et s'est terminée 13 000 ans avant JC. Essentiellement, ce régime essaie de manger comme un homme des cavernes.

Le régime paléo est basé sur le fait que la plupart des aliments auxquels nous sommes habitués sont apparus littéralement au cours des cent dernières années. Dans le même temps, les recherches scientifiques confirment qu'une alimentation riche en glucides raffinés perturbe le métabolisme en général, et le cerveau en particulier.

D'un point de vue pratique, le paléo est un régime efficace pour perdre du poids et maintenir un poids corporel stable. De plus, étant donné qu'un tel régime implique d'éviter les céréales (blé, seigle, avoine, riz), le paléo peut être un exemple de régime céto sans glucides.

L'avantage du régime paléo est qu'il convient à la nutrition en présence de maladies auto-immunes, telles que la polyarthrite rhumatoïde et le psoriasis. Si souvent, c'est la nourriture inadaptée qui devient la cause de l'exacerbation de telles maladies. C'est parce que le corps y réagit avec une réaction brutale du système immunitaire.

Le protocole paléo-auto-immun, appelé AIP en abrégé, introduit des choix alimentaires et de style de vie pour optimiser la fonction gastro-intestinale. Rappelons que l'intestin est le principal organe du système immunitaire. Contrairement au régime paléo ordinaire, il existe une liste plus restrictive d'aliments autorisés.

RECETTES DE PETIT DÉJEUNER PALÉO

1. Cuire des petits pains blancs

Ingrédients

- 250 ml de lait d'amande
- 10 g de levure sèche
- 230 g de farine de manioc (nous avons utilisé Ruut)
- 30 g de farine d'arrow-root ou de fécule de tapioca

- 15 g d'enveloppes de psyllium (assurez-vous d'en utiliser des moulues !)
- 1 pincée(s) de sel
- 2 oeufs
- 1 cuillère à soupe d'huile d'olive
- 1 cuillère à café de miel

préparation

1. Faites chauffer un peu le lait d'amande (environ 45 degrés). Mélanger le lait tiède avec la levure jusqu'à ce que la levure soit dissoute. Nous avons utilisé un mousseur à lait pour que la masse soit exempte de grumeaux. Laissez ensuite le mélange reposer pendant environ 15 minutes jusqu'à ce que des bulles se forment.
2. Mélanger 80 g de farine de manioc, la farine d'arrow-root, les cosses de psyllium et le sel. Ajouter le mélange sec au mélange de levure humide et mélanger dans une pâte. Ajouter un œuf, séparer le deuxième œuf et ajouter les jaunes. Réserver les blancs d'œufs. Ajouter également l'huile d'olive et mélanger.
3. Ajoutez maintenant le reste de la farine et pétrissez à la main en une boule de pâte. La pâte doit être légèrement collante. En cas de

doute, ajoutez plus de farine (si trop humide) ou plus d'huile (si trop sèche).

4. Façonner la pâte en 4 rouleaux. Couvrir d'un linge et laisser lever environ 1 heure.

5. Préchauffer le four à 200 degrés chaleur voûte/ sole.

6. Mélanger le blanc d'œuf restant avec le miel et 1 cuillère à café d'eau froide. Badigeonnez ensuite les rouleaux avec. Maintenant, coupez chaque petit pain dans le sens de la longueur.

7. Mettre au four pendant 25 minutes.

2. Salade de fruits d'été

Ingrédients

- 1 orange
- ½ citron
- 1 papaye
- 1 mangue
- 200 g de melon miel (1 pièce)
- ½ ananas
- 150 g de physalis
- 150g de fraises

Étapes de préparation

1. Pressez les moitiés d'orange et de citron. Épluchez la papaye, la mangue et la moitié de l'ananas.

2. Coupez et épépinez la papaye et coupez la chair en petits morceaux. Retirer la tige dure de l'ananas; Couper la pulpe en cubes de 1 cm. Coupez la pulpe de mangue vers le bas. Pelez et épépinez le melon. Lancez les deux dés.

3. Nettoyer et laver le physalis. Lavez et nettoyez les fraises et coupez-les en deux ou en quatre. Mélangez les fruits avec du jus d'orange et de citron dans un bol et servez, par exemple, dans des petits bols.

3. Arrot Pain à la Noix de Coco

Ingrédients

- 3 carottes (grosses)
- 5 œufs
- 4 cuillères à soupe de farine de noix de coco
- 4 cuillères à soupe d'huile de noix de coco
- 2 cuillères à soupe de noix de coco râpée
- 2 cuillères à soupe de sirop d'érable (éventuellement du miel)
- 1 cuillère à soupe de cannelle
- 0,5 cuillère à café de muscade
- 0,5 cuillère à café de vanille râpée
- 1 cuillère à café de levure de tartre
- 0,5 pincée(s) de sel

- Accessoires de cuisine
- Robot culinaire
- Râpe de cuisine
- Plat de cuisson boîte

préparation

1. Préchauffer le four à four ventilé à 175°C.
2. Épluchez les carottes et râpez-les en fines lamelles avec une râpe ou un robot culinaire. Mettre de côté.
3. Battre les œufs dans un bol, fouetter au batteur et ajouter progressivement la farine de noix de coco pour ne pas faire de grumeaux.
4. Faites fondre l'huile de coco (au four ou au micro-ondes) et utilisez-en un peu pour graisser un moule à pain. Ajouter le reste de l'huile de coco à la pâte.
5. Maintenant, ajoutez également de la noix de coco desséchée, du sirop d'érable, des épices et de la levure chimique. Bien fouetter le tout. Incorporez ensuite les carottes.
6. Versez la pâte dans le moule à pain, placez-la au milieu et sur la grille inférieure du four et faites cuire environ 25 à 30 minutes jusqu'à ce que le test du cure-dent soit réussi.

7. Sortir du four, laisser refroidir et couper en morceaux ou tranches (selon la largeur du pain).

4. Bouillon de petit-déjeuner épicé

Ingrédients

- 400 ml de bouillon d'os
- 2 cm de gingembre
- 1 bâton de cannelle
- 1 anis étoilé
- 1 cuillère à soupe d'huile de coco (facultatif)

Accessoires de cuisine

- mixer

préparation

1. Eplucher et couper grossièrement le gingembre.
2. Laissez mijoter le bâton de cannelle, l'anis étoilé et le gingembre avec le bouillon d'os pendant environ 10 minutes.
3. Retirez le bâton de cannelle et l'anis étoilé.
4. Versez le bouillon dans le mixeur (avec le gingembre). Ajouter éventuellement de l'huile de coco. Allumez brièvement le mélangeur sur le réglage le plus élevé jusqu'à ce que le gingembre soit râpé.
5. Versez dans des verres et dégustez.

5. Confiture de citrouille

Ingrédients

- 500 g de courge butternut
- 100 ml d'eau
- 1 bâton de cannelle
- 50 cl de lait de coco
- 1,5 cuillère à soupe de miel
- 1/2 citron (zeste et jus)
- 0,5 cuillère à café de cannelle moulue
- 1 cuillère à café de gélatine de boeuf (facultatif)

préparation

1. Pelez et épépinez le potiron et coupez-le en petits cubes.

2. Porter le potiron et l'eau à ébullition dans une casserole, ajouter le bâton de cannelle, laisser mijoter le tout ensemble. Après environ 15 minutes, ajoutez le lait de coco. Remuer plusieurs fois et ajouter un peu plus d'eau si nécessaire. Cuire encore 5-15 minutes - jusqu'à ce que la citrouille soit belle et douce.

3. Maintenant, retirez le bâton de cannelle et réduisez en purée la citrouille molle uniformément. Ensuite, incorporez le miel, le zeste de citron, le jus de citron et la cannelle moulue.

4. Si la consistance n'est pas assez épaisse, $\frac{1}{2}$ à 1 cuillère à café de gélatine de bœuf peut être ajoutée en option.

5. Versez la confiture encore chaude dans des pots à confiture soigneusement rincés à l'eau chaude et refermez aussitôt hermétiquement avec le couvercle.

6. La confiture se conserve au moins 1 semaine au réfrigérateur après ouverture.

6. Porridge aux pommes et à la cannelle

Ingrédients

- 2 pommes
- 200 ml de lait de noix
- 3 cuillères à soupe de graines de lin concassées
- 3 cuillères à soupe de noisettes moulues
- 3 cuillères à soupe de farine de noix
- 1 cuillère à café de cannelle
- 1 cuillère à soupe de miel

préparation

1. Lavez les pommes. Coupez une pomme en morceaux de la taille d'une bouchée, épluchez et râpez grossièrement l'autre pomme.
2. Faites chauffer le lait de noix dans une casserole.
3. Ajouter les graines de lin, les noisettes, la farine de noix, la cannelle et la pomme moulue et laisser mijoter environ 5 minutes en remuant à plusieurs reprises. Retirez ensuite du feu et laissez infuser encore 5 minutes.
4. Incorporer le miel.
5. Garnir la bouillie finie de morceaux de pomme et saupoudrer de cannelle sur le dessus.

7. Pain aux bananes paléo

Ingrédients

- 4 bananes
- 3 oeufs
- 1 cuillère à café de vanille en poudre
- 1 cuillère à soupe de miel
- 2 cuillères à soupe d'huile de noix de coco
- 200 g d'amandes en poudre
- 1 pincée(s) de gros sel de mer
- 1 cuillère à café de levure de tartre
- 1 cuillère à café de cannelle (au goût)

préparation

1. Fouetter les bananes, les œufs, la vanille, le miel et la graisse dans un bol à mélanger
2. Mélanger les amandes moulues, le sel et la levure et bien mélanger ou pétrir
3. Étaler la pâte dans un moule à cake
4. Placer dans le four préchauffé et cuire à 180 degrés pendant environ 35 minutes jusqu'à ce que le degré de brunissement souhaité soit atteint
5. Retirer du four et laisser refroidir

8. Style d'omelette sucrée

Ingrédients

- 6 dates
- 0,5 cuillère à café de cannelle
- 0,5 cuillère à café de gingembre en poudre
- 4 œufs
- 2 cuillères à soupe de lait d'amande
- 1 pincée(s) de sel
- 1 cuillère à soupe de beurre ou d'huile de coco

préparation

1. Tout d'abord, notez les dates.
2. Mettez 3-4 cuillères à soupe d'eau dans un petit bol et incorporez la cannelle et le

gingembre. Ajoutez les dattes et laissez-les ramollir environ 5 minutes.

3. Dans une tasse, battre les œufs avec le lait d'amande et le sel.

4. Faites chauffer le beurre dans une poêle anti-adhésive et laissez les dattes caraméliser dedans (sans liquide) pendant environ 1-2 minutes.

5. Versez ensuite le mélange d'œufs dessus et faites cuire à couvert à feu doux pendant environ 6 à 8 minutes jusqu'à ce que l'œuf soit complètement pris.

9. Pain aux tomates méditerranéen

Ingrédients

- 2 cuillères à soupe de farine de lin
- 150g de graines de tournesol
- 100g de pignons de pin
- 2 cuillères à soupe de ghee
- 1 cuillère à soupe de tahiné
- 4 œufs
- 2 cuillères à café de levure de tartre
- 0,5 cuillère à café de sel
- 0,5 cuillère à café de poudre d'oignon
- 1 pincée(s) de romarin
- 10 tomates séchées, hachées

préparation

1. Préchauffer le four à 180 degrés.
2. Transformez 120 g de graines de tournesol et 40 g de pignons de pin en farine au robot culinaire ou au mixeur plongeant. Ajouter le reste des grains (entiers) (= 30 g de graines de tournesol et 60 g de pignons).
3. Ajouter la farine de graines de lin, le tahini, le ghee (fondu), les œufs, la levure chimique, le sel, la poudre d'oignon, le romarin, les tomates hachées et pétrir pour former une pâte.
4. Tapisser le moule à pain de papier sulfurisé ou bien le graisser et verser la pâte dans le moule.
5. Mettre au four 40 minutes et faire le « stick test » de temps en temps vers la fin : Si la pâte ne colle plus au cure-dent, le pain est prêt.
6. Retirer du moule et laisser refroidir.

10. Crêpes vertes

Ingrédients

- 4 œufs
- 70 g de farine de châtaigne
- 2 poignées d'épinards frais
- 1 poignée de roquette
- 0,5 cuillère à café de sel
- 1 pincée(s) de poivre
- 1 pincée(s) de muscade
- Ghee pour la friture

préparation

1. Lavez les épinards et la roquette et essorez-les.

2. Mixer tous les ingrédients ensemble dans un mélangeur jusqu'à consistance crémeuse.

3. Faites chauffer un peu de ghee dans une poêle et faites cuire les crêpes de chaque côté pendant environ 2-3 minutes à feu moyen.

RECETTES DE DÉJEUNER PALÉO

11. Filet de poisson à la vapeur

Ingrédients

- 1 échalote
- $\frac{1}{2}$ tubercule de fenouil
- 60 g de petites carottes (1 petite carotte)
- 3 cuillères à soupe de bouillon de légumes classique
- sel
- poivre
- 70 g de filet de pangasius (pangasius bio de préférence)

- 2 tiges de persil plat
- ½ petit citron vert

Étapes de préparation

1. Épluchez et émincez finement l'échalote.
2. Nettoyez et lavez le fenouil et la carotte, épluchez finement la carotte. Couper les deux légumes en bâtonnets étroits.
3. Faites chauffer le bouillon dans une poêle enduite. Ajouter l'échalote, le fenouil et la carotte et cuire environ 3 minutes. Assaisonner au goût avec du sel et du poivre.
4. Rincez le filet de poisson, essuyez-le, salez légèrement et placez-le sur les légumes. Couvrir et cuire à feu doux pendant 8 à 10 minutes.
5. Pendant ce temps, lavez le persil, secouez-le pour le sécher, arrachez les feuilles et hachez-le finement avec un grand couteau.
6. Pressez un demi-citron vert et versez le jus sur le poisson au goût. Poivrer au goût, saupoudrer de persil et servir.

12. Goulasch au paprika aux oignons

Ingrédients

- 300 g d'oignons (6 oignons)
- 3 gousses d'ail
- 1 kg de boeuf (épaule)
- 3 cuillères à soupe d'huile de colza
- 2 cuillères à soupe de paprika noble doux
- 2 cuillères à soupe de poudre de paprika rose vif
- sel
- poivre
- 1 cuillère à café de graines de carvi moulues

- 20 g de concentré de tomate (1 cuillère à soupe)
- 1 l de bouillon de boeuf
- 2 poivrons rouges
- 2 poivrons jaunes
- 2 poivrons verts

Étapes de préparation

1. Eplucher et émincer les oignons et l'ail.
2. Rincez la viande sous l'eau froide, essuyez-la et coupez-la grossièrement en dés.
3. Faire chauffer l'huile dans une casserole. Faites-y revenir la viande par portions à feu vif et retirez-la à nouveau. Ensuite, mettez toute la viande dans la casserole, mélangez les oignons et l'ail et faites revenir le tout à feu vif pendant environ 3 minutes.
4. Incorporer la poudre de paprika, assaisonner avec du sel, du poivre et des graines de carvi et incorporer la pâte de tomate. Verser le bouillon de boeuf et couvrir et laisser mijoter environ 1 heure à feu doux.
5. Pendant ce temps, lavez et nettoyez les poivrons et coupez-les en lanières. Ensuite, ajoutez les lanières de paprika à la viande et laissez mijoter encore 30 minutes.

6. Assaisonner le goulasch avec du sel et du poivre.

13. Brochettes de chachlik grillées

Ingrédients

- 500 g de filet de porc
- 1 poivron vert
- 1 poivron jaune
- 1 poivron rouge
- 4 échalotes plates
- sel
- poivre fraîchement moulu

- 1 cuillère à soupe d'huile de tournesol

Étapes de préparation

1. Trempez d'abord les brochettes en bois dans l'eau.
2. Lavez la viande, essuyez-la et coupez-la en morceaux de la taille d'une bouchée. Couper en deux, épépiner, laver et couper les poivrons en morceaux. Eplucher les échalotes.
3. Placer la viande et le paprika en alternance sur 4 brochettes en bois et mettre une échalote à chaque extrémité. Saler et poivrer et badigeonner d'un peu d'huile. Faire griller sur le gril chaud en tournant jusqu'à ce qu'elles soient dorées pendant environ 10 minutes. Servir les brochettes de chachlik grillées.

14. Soupe au poulet et noix de coco du wok

Ingrédients

- 400 g de filet de poitrine de poulet
- poivre du moulin
- 3 carottes
- 1 tige de citronnelle
- 2 feuilles de lime kaffir
- 1 oignon de printemps
- 1 oignon
- 10 g de gingembre (1 pièce)
- 500 ml de bouillon de légumes
- 2 cuillères à soupe d'huile de sésame
- 400 ml de bouillon de volaille
- 200 ml de lait de coco

- 1 piment
- pimpinelle pour la garniture

Étapes de préparation

1. Rincez les filets de poulet, séchez-les avec du papier absorbant et coupez-les en lanières. Assaisonner de poivre. Lavez, épluchez et émincez finement les carottes. Ensuite, lavez et nettoyez les oignons nouveaux et coupez-les en rondelles. Coupez également la citronnelle très finement. Enfin, lavez les feuilles de citron vert et marquez légèrement.

2. Peler et couper en deux l'oignon et le couper en fines lamelles. Eplucher et hacher le gingembre. Couper le piment en deux dans le sens de la longueur, retirer le cœur, laver et hacher. Faites chauffer l'huile dans le wok. Ajouter les carottes, les oignons nouveaux, la citronnelle, la feuille de citron vert, l'oignon et le gingembre et faire revenir 3 à 4 minutes à feu moyen. Verser le bouillon de légumes et le bouillon de volaille et laisser mijoter environ 5 minutes.

3. Ajouter les lanières de poulet et laisser mijoter encore 10 minutes. Verser le lait de

coco, laisser mijoter encore 2 minutes puis assaisonner la soupe avec du piment. Lavez la pimpinelle, essorez-la et arrachez les feuilles. Portionner la soupe et servir garnie de pimpinelle.

15. Truite grillée au fenouil

Ingrédients

- 8 petites truites
- 4 citrons
- 4 tubercules de fenouil
- 1 bouquet d'aneth

- ½ frette de ciboulette
- ½ frette persil
- ½ frette livèche
- 1 branche de romarin
- sel de mer poivre
- herbes pour la garniture

Étapes de préparation

1. Lavez 2 citrons, frottez un peu de zeste et pressez bien les citrons. Mélanger le zeste de citron avec le jus et assaisonner de sel et de poivre. Ensuite, lavez les bulbes de fenouil, coupez-les en deux et placez la surface coupée dans le mélange de citron, laissez infuser. Pendant ce temps, laver les herbes, secouer pour sécher, arracher les aiguilles du romarin, mélanger les herbes restantes en 8 petits bouquets, emballer.

2. Lavez soigneusement la truite à l'intérieur et à l'extérieur sous l'eau courante, séchez-la et frottez-la avec un peu de sel. Retirez les bulbes de fenouil du mélange de citron. Tirez les herbes dans le mélange de citron et collez un bouquet de chacune dans le ventre d'une truite, ajoutez quelques aiguilles de romarin. Fermez les rabats du ventre avec une

brochette en bois. Lorsque toutes les truites sont remplies, arrosez-les du reste de marinade au citron, salez et poivrez à nouveau.

3. Faites griller le fenouil et la truite sur la grille chaude des deux côtés pendant un total de 10 à 15 minutes. Pendant ce temps, garnir les assiettes d'un demi-citron et d'herbes. Déposer deux poissons dessus et servir chaud.

16. Brochettes de poisson marocaines

Ingrédients

- ½ cuillère à café de graines de coriandre

- 1 cuillère à café de cumin
- 5 grains de poivre noir
- 2 piments forts séchés
- 0,1 g de fils de safran (1 sachet)
- oignon
- gousses d'ail
- 1 bouquet de coriandre fraîche
- 1 citron vert
- 1 cuillère à soupe de vinaigre de vin rouge
- à soupe d'huile d'olive
- sel de mer
- 400 g de filet de loche
- 200 g de filet d'espadon

Étapes de préparation

1. Brochettes de poisson marocaines préparation étape 1
2. Faites griller les graines de coriandre, le cumin et les grains de poivre dans une poêle jusqu'à ce qu'une fumée aromatique s'élève.
3. Brochettes de poisson marocaines préparation étape 2
4. Broyer finement avec les piments séchés et les fils de safran dans un mortier ou un hachoir éclair.

5. Brochettes de poisson marocaines préparation étape 3

6. Peler l'oignon et l'ail et les hacher finement. Laver la coriandre, la secouer pour la sécher. Cueillir les feuilles et hacher finement.

7. Brochettes de poisson marocaines préparation étape 4

8. Pressez le citron vert. Mélanger les épices moulues, les oignons, l'ail et la coriandre dans un bol avec 3 cuillères à soupe de jus de citron vert, le vinaigre et l'huile d'olive pour former un mélange d'assaisonnement (chermoula) et assaisonner de sel.

9. Brochettes de poisson marocaines préparation étape 5

10. Rincez les filets de poisson, essuyez-les et coupez-les chacun en env. cubes de 2 cm. Retourner le poisson dans environ 2/3 de la chermoula et laisser mariner au réfrigérateur pendant au moins 1-2 heures.

11. Brochettes de poisson marocaines préparation étape 6

12. Placez les morceaux de poisson sur 4 longues brochettes en bois et faites-les griller sur du charbon de bois à feu moyen ou dans une

lèchefrite pendant 2 minutes de chaque côté.
Servir avec la chermoula restante.

17. Mâche aux noix

Ingrédients

- 1 petit oignon rouge
- 1 cuillère à soupe de persil haché
- sel
- poivre
- $\frac{1}{2}$ cuillère à café de moutarde

- 1 cc de vinaigre de vin blanc
- 3 cuillères à soupe d'huile d'olive
- 100 g de mâche
- 6 tomates cerises
- 1 tranche de jambon cuit
- 2 cuillères à soupe de cerneaux de noix hachés

Étapes de préparation

1. Eplucher l'oignon et le couper en fins cubes. Mélanger le persil et l'oignon coupé en dés dans un bol avec du sel, du poivre, de la moutarde et du vinaigre. Incorporer progressivement l'huile d'olive au fouet.
2. Laver, nettoyer, trier et essorer la mâche. Laver les tomates et les couper en deux. Tourner la mâche et les tomates dans la vinaigrette et les disposer sur des assiettes. Couper le jambon cuit en fines lanières et saupoudrer de noix sur la mâche. Sers immédiatement.

18. Tortilla aux épinards

Ingrédients

- 350 g de feuilles d'épinards
- sel
- 1 poivron rouge
- 1 oignon végétal
- 2 gousses d'ail
- 50 g d'amandes en grains
- 5 œufs
- 100 ml d'eau minérale
- poivre
- Noix de muscade

- 15 g de ghee (beurre clarifié ; 1 cuillère à soupe)

Étapes de préparation

1. Lavez les épinards, essorez-les, blanchissez-les dans de l'eau bouillante salée pendant 1 minute. Égoutter, tremper à froid, bien exprimer.
2. Lavez, nettoyez et émincez le poivron.
3. Peler l'oignon et l'ail et les hacher finement. Hacher grossièrement les amandes.
4. Fouetter les œufs avec de l'eau minérale, assaisonner avec du sel, du poivre et de la muscade fraîchement râpée.
5. Faites fondre le ghee dans une grande poêle allant au four. Y faire revenir l'oignon et l'ail à feu moyen pendant 1 à 2 minutes jusqu'à ce qu'ils soient translucides. Ajouter le paprika et les épinards et verser le mélange d'œufs dessus. Ajouter les amandes et laisser reposer 2 minutes.
6. Cuire la tortilla dans un four préchauffé à 200°C (chaleur tournante 180°C ; gaz : niveau 3) pendant 10-15 minutes jusqu'à ce qu'elle soit dorée.
7. Retirer et servir coupé en morceaux.

19. Curry de Porc et Pêche

Ingrédients

- 100g de raisins secs
- 2 ½ cm de gingembre frais
- 1 échalote
- 600 g de porc maigre de cuisse, prêt à cuire
- 2 cuillères à soupe d'huile végétale
- 2 cuillères à soupe de pâte de curry rouge
- 150 ml de soupe à la viande
- 400 ml de lait de coco non sucré
- sel

- poivre du moulin
- 6 pêches
- 4 oignons nouveaux

Étapes de préparation

1. Faire tremper les raisins secs dans de l'eau tiède.
2. Pelez et hachez finement le gingembre et l'échalote.
3. Lavez la viande, essuyez-la, parez-la et coupez-la en morceaux de la taille d'une bouchée.
4. Faites chauffer l'huile dans une casserole et faites revenir la viande par portions. Ajouter l'oignon et le gingembre, ajouter la viande et incorporer la pâte de curry. Déglacer avec le bouillon et le lait de coco, incorporer les raisins secs égouttés, saler et poivrer et laisser mijoter à feu moyen pendant environ 15 minutes.
5. Pendant ce temps, ébouillantez les pêches, éteignez, épluchez, coupez en deux, dénoyautez et coupez en quartiers étroits. Lavez et nettoyez les oignons nouveaux et coupez-les en fines rondelles.

6. Ajouter les quartiers de pêche au curry, laisser mijoter encore 3-4 minutes, assaisonner au goût et servir parsemé de rondelles d'oignon.

20. Curry de crevettes

Ingrédients

- 1 boîte de lait de coco 400 ml
- 200 g de crevettes prêtes à cuire
- 200 ml de bouillon de poulet
- 1 cuillère à soupe bombée de pâte de curry jaune asia shop
- 1 poivron vert
- 1 gros oignon blanc
- 2 gousses d'ail
- ½ tige de poireau
- huile de sésame

- sel

Étapes de préparation

1. Lavez les poivrons, coupez-les en deux, épépinez-les et coupez-les en très petits cubes. Peler l'oignon et l'ail et les hacher finement. Nettoyer le poireau, le couper en deux et le couper en fines lamelles.

2. Faites chauffer 2 cuillères à soupe d'huile et faites revenir l'oignon et l'ail jusqu'à ce qu'ils soient translucides. Ajouter la pâte de curry et faire revenir brièvement. Éteindre avec du bouillon de volaille. Ajouter le paprika et le poireau et cuire à couvert pendant 5-6 minutes à feu moyen. Ajouter le lait de coco et laisser mijoter (sans couvercle) encore 10 minutes. Ajouter les crevettes et laisser mijoter 3 minutes à feu doux plus que de les laisser cuire. Assaisonner au goût avec du sel et servir immédiatement si désiré dans des moitiés de noix de coco préparées.

RECETTES DESSERTS PALEO

21. Carpaccio de papaye au pesto de menthe

Ingrédients

- 200 g de petite papaye mûre (1 petite papaye mûre)
- $\frac{1}{2}$ citron vert bio
- 8 grandes feuilles de menthe
- 3 noix de cajou

Étapes de préparation

1. Coupez la papaye en deux dans le sens de la longueur et évidez-la avec une cuillère à café.

2. Eplucher les moitiés de papaye et couper la pulpe en tranches de 1 cm d'épaisseur.

3. Rincez le citron vert à l'eau chaude et frottez-le pour le sécher. Peler la peau très finement à l'aide d'un économe et la couper en très fines lamelles (julienne).

4. Hacher finement la moitié des lamelles de citron vert.

5. Pressez le citron vert et versez 1 à 2 cuillères à café de jus sur les lamelles de papaye.

6. Laver la menthe, la secouer pour la sécher et mettre quelques feuilles de côté. Hacher finement le reste, broyer avec le zeste de citron vert haché et 1 cuillère à café d'eau dans un mortier en une pâte fine.

7. Hacher les noix de cajou et les incorporer au pesto à la menthe.

8. Disposez la papaye de manière décorative sur une assiette et versez le pesto dessus. Garnir de feuilles de menthe et de julienne de citron vert.

22. Fruits thaïs grillés

Ingrédients

- 4 tiges de citronnelle
- 15 g de gingembre (1 pièce)
- 1 citron vert bio
- 1 cuillère à soupe de miel liquide
- 100 g de petite carambole (1 petite carambole)
- 8 physalis
- 200 g de papaye (0,5 papaye)
- 100 g d'ananas frais

Étapes de préparation

1. Lavez et nettoyez la citronnelle et coupez les bâtonnets en deux dans le sens de la longueur. Pelez le gingembre et râpez-le finement.
2. Rincez le citron vert à l'eau chaude, séchez-le et décollez quelques bandes de peau très fines avec une fermeture éclair zeste.
3. Couper le citron vert en deux, presser et mélanger le jus avec le gingembre et le miel dans un petit bol
4. Lavez la carambole, essuyez-la et coupez-la en tranches. Retirez les physalis des gousses, lavez-les et séchez-les.
5. Coupez l'ananas en morceaux de la taille d'une bouchée. Retirez les graines de la moitié de papaye avec une cuillère à soupe; Épluchez la papaye et coupez-la en morceaux de la taille d'une bouchée.
6. Tapisser une plaque à pâtisserie de papier sulfurisé. Placer les fruits en alternance sur les brochettes de citronnelle, badigeonner avec le mélange citron vert-miel et disposer sur la plaque de cuisson.
7. Faites griller les brochettes de fruits sous le gril du four préchauffé pendant 5 à 8 minutes jusqu'à ce que les bords des fruits deviennent brun clair, en les retournant une fois.

Parsemez les brochettes de lamelles de zeste de citron vert et servez aussitôt.

23. Salade de melon aux pistaches

Ingrédients

- 1 kg de petite pastèque (1 petite pastèque)
- 60 g de dattes (6 dattes)
- 1 citron vert
- 2 cuillères à soupe de sirop d'agave
- 40 g de pistaches hachées
- 4 tiges de menthe

Étapes de préparation

1. Coupez la pastèque en deux et utilisez un emporte-pièce parisien pour découper des petites boules. Evidez les dattes et coupez-les en morceaux. Pressez le citron vert. Mélanger les dattes avec le jus de citron vert et le sirop d'agave et mélanger aux boules de melon. Laissez infuser au réfrigérateur pendant environ 20 minutes.
2. Laver la menthe, la secouer pour la sécher et arracher les feuilles. Répartir la salade dans des bols, saupoudrer de pistaches et servir garni de menthe.

24. Salade d'orange et pamplemousse

Ingrédients

- 125 g petite orange bio (1 petite orange bio)
- 175 g petit pamplemousse rose (qualité bio, 1 petit pamplemousse rose)
- 1 datte séchée

Étapes de préparation

1. Rincer l'orange et le pamplemousse à l'eau chaude et les sécher.
2. À l'aide d'un économe, prélevez env. Bande de 3 cm de long de pelure très fine des deux fruits et coupée en fines lanières.

3. Pelez l'orange et le pamplemousse si épais que la peau blanche est également enlevée.

4. Découper les filets de fruits entre les peaux séparatrices ; travailler au-dessus d'un bol et récupérer le jus.

5. Coupez la datte en deux dans le sens de la longueur, retirez le noyau si besoin, coupez la pulpe en très fines lamelles.

6. Mélanger les lamelles de dattes avec les filets de fruits, la moitié des lamelles d'écorces et le jus capturé dans un bol. Laissez infuser 10 minutes. Ensuite, dresser sur une assiette et parsemer des lamelles de zeste restantes.

25. salade de fruits frais

Ingrédients

- $\frac{1}{2}$ mangue
- 200 g de baies mélangées
- 50 g de raisins rouges
- $\frac{1}{2}$ pamplemousse
- $\frac{1}{2}$ citron vert bio
- $\frac{1}{2}$ pomme
- 4 cuillères à soupe de jus de citron
- 1 cuillère à soupe de miel
- 5 cuillères à soupe de pistaches hachées

Étapes de préparation

1. Pelez la mangue, coupez le noyau et coupez-la en filets. Laver les baies et les raisins, fileter le pamplemousse. Lavez le citron vert et coupez-le en tranches. Lavez la pomme, retirez le trognon et coupez-la en quartiers.

2. Mélanger le jus de citron avec le miel et les pistaches. Préparez 4 bols et répartissez les fruits préparés sur le dessus. Nappez de sauce et servez aussitôt.

26. Salade de melons

Ingrédients

- $\frac{1}{2}$ pastèque
- $\frac{1}{2}$ melon au sucre
- $\frac{1}{2}$ melon miel
- 1 pomme
- 1 petit citron (jus)
- 1 cuillère à café de miel

Étapes de préparation

1. Découpez des petites boules dans les moitiés de melon à l'aide d'un emporte-pièce parisienne.
2. Mélanger le jus de citron avec le miel et mélanger dans les boules de melon. Couvrir et

laisser reposer au réfrigérateur pendant env. 30 minutes.

3. Lavez et coupez la pomme en quartiers, enlevez le trognon et coupez-la en fins quartiers.

4. Répartir les boules de melon dans quatre verres et servir décoré des quartiers de pommes.

27. Brochettes de fruits

Ingrédients

- 150g de fraises
- 2 nectarines mûres
- 1 pomme verte zb granny smith
- 200 g de pastèque
- 200 g de pulpe de melon miel
- 200 g de pulpe de melon cantaloup
- 1 citron
- 1 cuillère à soupe de miel liquide

Étapes de préparation

1. Lavez et nettoyez les fraises et les nectarines. Coupez les nectarines en deux, dénoyautez-les et coupez-les en quartiers. Pelez et coupez la pomme en quatre, retirez le trognon et coupez-la en morceaux de la taille d'une bouchée.

2. Aussi, divisez la pulpe de melon en morceaux de la taille d'une bouchée et mélangez avec le reste des fruits, pressez le citron, ajoutez aux fruits avec du miel et laissez infuser pendant environ 1 heure. Puis les coller en alternance sur des brochettes en bois et servir sur une assiette.

28. salade de fruits exotiques

Ingrédients

- 1 ananas
- 1 kiwi
- 1 orange
- 2 cuillères à soupe de miel liquide
- cc de cannelle
- cc de cardamome moulue
- 1 grenade

Étapes de préparation

1. Épluchez l'ananas à l'aide d'un couteau bien aiguisé, coupez-le en quatre dans le sens de la

longueur, retirez la tige et coupez la chair en petits morceaux. Épluchez le kiwi, coupez-le en deux dans le sens de la longueur et coupez-le en fines tranches.

2. Couper l'orange en deux et presser le jus. Mélanger du jus d'orange avec du miel, de la cannelle et de la cardamome et mélanger avec de l'ananas et du kiwi.

3. Coupez la grenade en deux et retirez les noyaux des fruits. Disposer la salade dans des assiettes et saupoudrer les graines sur la salade de fruits.

29. Salade de fruits aux noisettes

Ingrédients

- 1 filet de melon
- 500g de fraises
- 1 citron vert
- 2 cuillères à soupe de miel
- 75g de noisettes

Étapes de préparation

1. Coupez le melon en deux et retirez les noyaux avec une cuillère. Retirez la chair du melon et coupez-le en morceaux.
2. Lavez et nettoyez les fraises et coupez-les en morceaux. Mélangez les fruits. Répartir le

miel dessus et laisser infuser un instant la salade de fruits.

3. Couper les noisettes en rondelles et parsemer sur la salade de fruits avant de servir.

30. Salade de pamplemousse

Ingrédients

- 2 pamplemousses
- 1 pomelo
- 2 oranges
- 2 cuillères à soupe de miel
- 20 ml de liqueur d'orange ou de jus de citron
- 1 grenade
- verveine citronnelle pour la garniture

Étapes de préparation

1. Pelez soigneusement tous les agrumes et découpez les filets. Presser le reste de la

pulpe et mélanger avec le miel et la liqueur. Mélanger avec les filets de fruits.

2. Pressez la grenade tout autour, coupez-la en deux et retirez les graines. Mélanger avec la laitue et répartir dans des bols.

3. Servir garni de verveine citronnée.

RECETTES DE BOISSONS ET SMOOTHIES PALEO

31. Cappuccino au lait d'amande

Ingrédients

- 30g de grains de café
- 200 ml d'eau
- 300 ml de lait d'amande

préparation

1. Moudre les grains de café sur le réglage de mouture le plus bas.

2. Versez de l'eau et du café en poudre dans la machine à expresso et portez à ébullition sur la cuisinière.
3. Pendant ce temps, faites chauffer le lait d'amande, divisez-le dans 2 grandes tasses et battez jusqu'à consistance crémeuse avec le mousseur à lait.
4. Répartir l'espresso entre les deux tasses.
5. Servir saupoudré d'épices (par exemple cacao, cannelle ou muscade).

32. Poêlée de choux de Savoie

Ingrédients

- 1 chou de Milan
- 1 oignon
- 1 gousse d'ail
- 2 cuillères à soupe de ghee
- 100 ml de bouillon de légumes
- 0,5 cuillère à café de sel
- 1 pincée(s) de poivre
- 1 pincée(s) de muscade

préparation

1. Coupez le chou frisé en quatre, ôtez la tige et coupez les feuilles en fines lanières.
2. Coupez également l'oignon en fines lamelles.
3. Hacher finement la gousse d'ail.

4. Faites chauffer le ghee dans une grande poêle et faites revenir l'oignon pendant environ 3 minutes jusqu'à ce qu'il soit translucide.
5. Ajouter l'ail et le chou de Milan et faire légèrement rôtir encore 5 minutes.
6. Déglacer avec le bouillon de légumes et cuire à couvert environ 15 minutes.
7. Assaisonnez avec du sel, du poivre et de la muscade et servez!

33. Smoothie à l'ortie

Ingrédients

- 1 poignée de pointes d'ortie
- 1 poignée de feuilles de menthe
- 1 poignée de feuilles de pissenlit
- 1 poire mûre
- 0,5 avocat
- 4 dattes dénoyautées
- Jus de 1/2 citron
- 500 ml d'eau
- 1 poignée de glaçons

préparation

1. Lavez bien les pointes d'ortie, le pissenlit et les feuilles de menthe et essuyez-les.
2. Lavez, épépinez et coupez la poire en gros morceaux.
3. Épépinez et épluchez l'avocat.
4. Mettez tous les ingrédients ensemble dans un mélangeur puissant et mélangez jusqu'à consistance crémeuse. Plus d'eau peut être ajoutée si nécessaire.

34. Smoothie aux superaliments

Ingrédients

- 1 pomme
- 150 g de baies mélangées de saison
- 5 morceaux de feuilles de menthe
- 50g de graines de tournesol
- 150 ml d'eau

préparation

1. Coupez et épépinez la pomme.
2. Lavez la menthe et les baies.
3. Mettez tous les ingrédients dans un mixeur et mixez au plus haut niveau pour former un smoothie onctueux.

4. Assaisonnez éventuellement avec un peu de jus de citron.

35. Smoothie à la citrouille sucrée

Ingrédients

- 1 citrouille d'Hokkaido
- 2 bananes
- 400 ml de lait de coco
- 2 cuillères à soupe de cannelle
- 2 cuillères à café de muscade râpée
- 1 cuillère à soupe de miel (facultatif)
- 1 cuillère à soupe de jus de citron (facultatif)

préparation

1. Faites chauffer 2-3 litres d'eau dans une grande casserole. Épluchez, coupez en quatre et épépinez le potiron et coupez-le en petits morceaux. Verser dans l'eau bouillante et laisser mijoter environ 10-12 minutes. (il doit être possible de couper le potiron avec une cuillère).
2. Égoutter les morceaux de citrouille et les placer dans le robot culinaire ou le batteur sur socle. Ajouter la banane, le lait de coco et les épices et réduire en purée jusqu'à formation d'un liquide buvable. Si vous aimez le smoothie à la citrouille plus froid, vous devez ajouter quelques glaçons supplémentaires et les écraser avec.
3. Assaisonnez le smoothie à la citrouille avec un peu de miel et de jus de citron, selon votre goût, et servez dans 2-3 grands verres.

36. Chai Latte à la vanille

Ingrédients

- 250 ml de thé rooibos
- 100 ml de lait d'amande
- 100 ml de lait de coco
- 1 cuillère à café de clous de girofle moulus
- 1 cuillère à café de cannelle
- 1 pincée(s) de vanille
- 2 cuillères à café de miel

préparation

1. Versez de l'eau bouillante sur le thé rooibos et laissez infuser pendant 8 minutes. Je le

fais beau et fort et utilise 3 cuillères à soupe
de thé en vrac dans 250 ml d'eau.

2. Mélanger le lait d'amande, le lait de coco et
   les épices dans une casserole et réchauffer.
   Faire mousser avec le mousseur à lait.

3. Répartir le thé dans 2 verres. Versez la
   mousse de lait et, selon votre goût, sucrez
   avec du miel.

37. Lait Doré

Ingrédients

- 1 morceau de gingembre
- 2 morceaux de curcuma
- 150 ml de lait de coco
- 150 ml de lait d'amande
- 1 cuillère à café de cannelle
- 1 pincée(s) de clou de girofle moulu
- 1 pincée(s) de poivre
- 2 cuillères à café de miel

préparation

1. Eplucher et couper grossièrement le gingembre et le curcuma.
2. Mettez le lait de coco et le lait d'amande dans une casserole.
3. Ajouter le gingembre, le curcuma, la cannelle et les clous de girofle moulus. Mélangez le tout et chauffez 5 minutes.
4. Mixez le tout et répartissez dans 2 verres. Saupoudrer de poivre frais et sucrer avec du miel au goût.

38. Smoothie Tropical

Ingrédients

- 1 orange
- 1 banane
- 0,5 ananas
- 1 poignée de coriandre

préparation

1. Pressez l'orange.
2. Lavez la coriandre et arrachez grossièrement les feuilles de la tige.

3. Retirez la peau et la tige de l'ananas et coupez-le en cubes.
4. Mettre le jus d'orange, la banane, l'ananas et la coriandre dans le mixeur

39. Café frappé à l'avocat

Ingrédients

- 1 morceau d'avocat mûr
- 180 ml de lait d'amande
- 6 glaçons
- 50 ml de café en grains entiers
- 1,5 cuillère à soupe de miel

- 2 cuillères à café de cannelle

préparation

1. Coupez l'avocat en deux, retirez le noyau et évidez la pulpe.
2. Bien mélanger tous les ingrédients jusqu'à l'obtention d'une consistance crémeuse. Ajouter des glaçons et mélanger à nouveau soigneusement. Si nécessaire, ajoutez du lait d'amande à la consistance désirée.
3. Répartir entre 2 verres.

40. Smoothie à la betterave et au chocolat

Ingrédients

- 1 betterave précuite
- 1 avocat
- 1 banane
- 2 poignées d'épinards
- 3 cuillères à café de cacao
- 1 cuillère à café de cannelle
- 1 cuillère à café de vanille
- 250 ml de jus d'orange (sans additifs)

préparation

1. Coupez et épépinez l'avocat et retirez la pulpe.

2. Mettez tous les ingrédients dans le mélangeur et transformez en un smoothie lisse.

3. Assaisonner de cacao et de cannelle.

4. Ajouter du jus d'orange selon la consistance désirée.

RECETTES D'ACCOMPAGNEMENT PALEO

41. Salade de pomme céleri

Ingrédients

- 1 céleri-rave
- 2 petites pommes boskop
- 2 cuillères à soupe de jus de citron
- 1 cuillère à café de vinaigre de cidre de pomme
- 1 cc d'huile de noix
- 2 cuillères à soupe d'amandes effilées
- 2 branches de persil

Étapes de préparation

1. Lavez la pomme, coupez-la en deux, retirez le trognon. Eplucher le céleri, enlever les points durs, râper grossièrement les deux. Mélanger le jus de citron avec le vinaigre et l'huile, mélanger à la salade.
2. Faire revenir les amandes dans une poêle sans matière grasse, saupoudrer dessus. Épluchez finement les feuilles de persil et saupoudrez-les également.

42. Salade d'avocat et coriandre au citron vert

Ingrédients

- 2 citrons verts
- 3 avocats
- ½ frette coriandre
- 1 petit piment vert
- sel
- poivre blanc

Étapes de préparation

1. Lavez les citrons verts sous l'eau chaude, séchez-les, frottez-en un peu, pressez les citrons verts.
2. Coupez les avocats en deux, retirez les noyaux. Coupez la pulpe en quartiers, enlevez la peau et coupez la pulpe en dés. Mélanger les cubes d'avocat avec le jus de citron vert.
3. Laver la coriandre, la secouer pour la sécher, la hacher grossièrement et la mélanger avec les cubes d'avocat. Ensuite, lavez le piment, coupez-le en deux, épépinez et retirez la peau intérieure blanche, coupez la pulpe en fins cubes.
4. Mélanger les cubes de piment à la salade. Saler et poivrer et laisser infuser environ 30 minutes. Servir légèrement frais.

43. salade de radis

Ingrédients

- 300 g de radis
- 300 g de radis noir radis d'hiver
- 1 concombre
- sel
- poivre du moulin fraîchement moulu

Étapes de préparation

1. Lavez et nettoyez les radis et coupez-les en tranches très fines ou en plan (trancheuse).

2. Laver le concombre et peler les longues lanières de pelure du concombre avec un zeste (ou peler finement la pelure à l'aide d'un économe et couper dans le sens de la longueur en lanières très fines).
3. Disposez les radis et les tranches de radis sur des assiettes ou des bols comme des tuiles, saupoudrez de sel et de poivre et ajoutez les lamelles de concombre de manière décorative.

44. Courgettes grillées aux olives

Ingrédients

- 4 petites courgettes
- 2 cuillères à soupe de beurre clarifié
- 100g d'olives noires
- 3 tiges de livèche
- 2 tiges de basilic
- 3 cuillères à soupe d'huile d'olive
- 5 cuillères à soupe de vinaigre
- 1 cuillère à soupe de bouillon de légumes
- sel
- poivre blanc

Étapes de préparation

1. Couper les courgettes en diagonale en tranches de 1 cm d'épaisseur. Chauffer une poêle à griller ou un grill et faire griller brièvement des deux côtés dans du beurre clarifié chaud.

2. Égoutter les olives. Lavez la livèche et le basilic, essorez-les et arrachez les feuilles des tiges. Mélanger avec le reste des ingrédients et laisser mariner au moins 45 minutes. Disposer sur une assiette et servir.

45. Légumes vapeur

Ingrédients

1. 200 g de fleurettes de chou-fleur
2. 200 g de fleurettes de brocoli
3. 100 g de cassonade
4. 200g de carottes
5. ½ frette de radis
6. sel
7. poivre du moulin

Étapes de préparation

1. Coupez les bouquets de chou-fleur et de brocoli plus petits si nécessaire et lavez-les.

Nettoyez les pois mange-tout, coupez les extrémités. Lavez et épluchez les carottes.

2. Lavez, nettoyez et émincez les radis.

3. Mettez le chou-fleur et les carottes dans un panier vapeur (en bambou) et mettez le couvercle. Porter de l'eau à ébullition dans un wok (ou une casserole adaptée) et couvrir les légumes et cuire à la vapeur pendant 6-8 minutes.

4. Retirer, saler et poivrer et incorporer le persil.

46. Salade de papaye au concombre

Ingrédients

- 900 g de papaye (2 papayes)
- 1 kg de concombre (2 concombres)
- 2 citrons bio
- 1 cuillère à soupe de miel de fleurs liquide
- 1 cuillère à soupe d'huile d'olive
- 3 tiges de menthe
- ½ frette de ciboulette
- sel

Étapes de préparation

1. Épluchez les papayes et coupez-les en quatre dans le sens de la longueur. Videz la pulpe et coupez-la en tranches d'environ 5 mm d'épaisseur. Transférer dans un grand bol.

2. Lavez et épluchez les concombres, coupez-les en deux dans le sens de la longueur et épépinez-les à l'aide d'une cuillère. Couper transversalement en tranches également d'environ 5 mm d'épaisseur et ajouter aux papayes.

3. Lavez 1 citron à l'eau chaude, séchez-le et râpez finement le zeste. Pelez les deux citrons si épais que la peau blanche est également enlevée.

4. Découpez les filets de citron entre les peaux séparatrices et coupez-les en deux. Ajouter les filets et le zeste de citron râpé au mélange de papaye et de concombre.

5. Mélanger le miel et l'huile d'olive dans un petit bol. Mélanger avec les filets de papaye, de concombre et de citron et laisser infuser la salade pendant environ 15 minutes.

6. Pendant ce temps, lavez la menthe et la ciboulette et secouez-les pour les sécher. Ensuite, arrachez les feuilles de menthe et coupez en lamelles, la ciboulette en rouleaux.

7. Ajouter la ciboulette et la menthe à la salade. Assaisonner avec un peu de sel et servir ou mettre dans un récipient de conservation des

aliments bien fermé (capacité d'environ 1,5 l) pour le transport.

47. Salade d'Avocat, Ananas et Concombres

Ingrédients

- 1 tranché concombre
- 3 tranches d'ananas (ananas)
- 1/2 oignon rouge en filet
- 2 avocats (avocats)
- 1/3 tasse d'huile d'olive
- 2 cuillères à soupe de jus de citron
- 1 sel de cuisine
- 1 piment cdita

Préparation

1. Couper l'avocat et l'ananas en cubes moyens.

2. Ensuite, coupez le concombre, retirez les graines avec une cuillère et coupez-le en tranches.
3. Mélangez ce qui précède dans un bol, ajoutez l'oignon rouge, salez, poivrez et assaisonnez avec de l'huile d'olive et du jus de citron.

48. Salade de mangue et avocat

Ingrédients

- 1 unité(s) de Laitue hachée
- 1 pincée de poivre
- 1 unité(s) d'Avocat
- 1 unité(s) de Mangue
- 1 cuillère à soupe de vinaigre de vin blanc
- 1 cuillère à soupe d'huile d'olive
- 2 cuillères à soupe d'amandes grillées hachées
- 2 cuillères à soupe de canneberges séchées
- sel

Préparation

1. Eplucher et hacher les légumes.

2. Mettez la laitue, la mangue, l'avocat, les amandes et les canneberges dans un bol.
3. D'autre part, mélangez l'huile avec le vinaigre et ajoutez du sel et du poivre.
4. Verser sur la salade et mélanger.
5. Servir dans les assiettes et déguster.

49. Salade d'asperges et tomates

Ingrédients
- 1 citron
- 1 oignon rouge
- 1 aneth
- 200g de tomates cerises
- 150 g de crevettes d'eau profonde (prêtes à cuire)
- 2 cuillères à soupe d'huile d'olive
- 1 cuillère à café de sirop d'agave ou de miel
- sel
- poivre noir
- 500g d'asperges blanches

Étapes de préparation

1. Pressez le citron. Eplucher l'oignon et le couper en fines lamelles. Lavez l'aneth, secouez-le et hachez-le. Laver les tomates et les couper en deux. Mettre le jus de citron, les oignons, l'aneth et les tomates dans un bol avec les crevettes, l'huile et le sirop d'agave. Salez, poivrez et mélangez bien.
2. Lavez les asperges et épluchez-les soigneusement avec l'économe. Coupez les extrémités ligneuses et coupez les bâtonnets en diagonale en tranches. Laissez les pointes d'asperges entières.
3. Portez à ébullition une casserole suffisamment grande avec de l'eau salée et faites-y cuire les asperges pendant 4 à 5 minutes jusqu'à ce qu'elles soient al dente.
4. Égoutter les asperges dans une passoire et bien égoutter.
5. Ajouter aux autres ingrédients encore chauds et bien mélanger. Laisser infuser 3 minutes, assaisonner à nouveau de sel et de poivre et servir.

50. Salade de tomates et menthe

Ingrédients

- 1 kg de tomates (différentes tailles ; en jaune et rouge)
- 1 poignée de menthe (5 g)
- 1 poignée de persil (5 g)
- 4 cuillères à soupe de vinaigre de vin blanc
- 4 cuillères à soupe d'huile d'olive
- sel
- poivre du moulin
- ½ cuillère à café de pul biber (épice chili)

Étapes de préparation

1. Laver les tomates et retirer les tiges. Coupez les tomates en deux, en quartiers ou en tranches, selon leur taille. Disposer les couleurs mélangées sur des assiettes. Rincer les herbes, secouer pour sécher, arracher les feuilles et les hacher grossièrement.

2. Pour la vinaigrette, mélanger le vinaigre avec l'huile, le sel et le poivre et assaisonner au goût. Arroser la salade et saupoudrer d'herbes. Raffinez avec Pul Biber et servez la salade de tomates et menthe.

CONCLUSION

Quiconque veut perdre du poids le fera certainement car grâce au régime paléo, il renonce au fast-food, à la pizza, à la farine blanche et au sucre et mange à la place du poisson et des légumes. Manger le plus naturellement possible a du sens dans tous les cas.

Mais : Le changement radical nécessaire avec le régime paléo nécessite de la volonté, du temps et de l'argent pour acheter des aliments de haute qualité et les préparer selon les règles paléo. Surtout, il peut être difficile de se passer de céréales - y compris les petits pains ou les plats de pâtes.

Les personnes intolérantes (auparavant inaperçues) peuvent bénéficier du régime paléo. Cependant, le régime paléo n'est pas une recommandation générale.

Lightning Source UK Ltd.
Milton Keynes UK
UKHW050955170921
390725UK00008B/157